CHOPIN
(*from a woodcut by Eric King*)

CHOPIN

by BASIL MAINE

A. A. WYN, INC.

NEW YORK, N.Y.

5713
___

CONTENTS

CHRONOLOGY

1810.... Birth : February 22.

1824.... Enters Warsaw Lyceum.

1829.... Concert at Vienna.

1830.... First Concert at Warsaw.

1830.... Leaves Poland.

1830.... Joins Kalkbrenner's classes.

1832.... First Concert in Paris.

1836.... End of Marja Wodzinska episode.

1837.... First visit to England.

1837.... With George Sand to Majorca.

1839.... At Nohant.

1842.... Concerts.

1847.... Breach with George Sand.

1848.... Last Concert in Paris.

1848.... In England and Scotland.

1849.... Death in Paris.

NOTES

1. I have retained the original spelling of Polish names throughout.

2. I wish to thank Mr. Desmond Harmsworth for allowing me to quote from his publication of Chopin's letters. (See Bibliography.)

B. M.

CHAPTER I

Birth of Chopin – childhood – friendships – first compositions.

AT the end of the eighteenth century Poland was passing through one of her many tragic periods. In 1772 Prussia, Austria and Russia had taken away some of her lands and, having gained a footing, these three neighbouring powers had no intention of losing ground. Russia was especially aggressive. All attempts by Poland to re-form herself were frustrated. When, in 1793, Russia and Prussia again prepared to divide the spoils, a climax was reached. In the following spring Poland gathered up her full strength for resistance. She continued the struggle for nearly a year but at the end lost almost everything, and her king abdicated.

Among those who joined the National Guard during this rising was Nicholas Chopin. This young man was born at Nancy and at the age of seventeen had come to Warsaw to take a position as cashier in a tobacco factory. In the National Guard he became a captain. Towards the end of the struggle of 1794 he was on duty with his company at Praga, a suburb of Warsaw. The company was relieved and a few hours later Praga was captured. In the present context this incident is of more than ordinary importance ; for twelve years later Nicholas Chopin, who had since become a tutor to the son of a countess, married Justina Krzyzanowska, a lady-in-waiting in the same household ; and four years after the marriage there was born to them their second child, a son whom they called Fryderyk.

The origin of Nicholas Chopin is uncertain. Some have said that he was of Polish blood; others that he was a Lorrainer. Some have recorded that he was descended from a Polish nobleman who had accompanied King Stanislas to Lorraine; others have attempted to trace his line of descent from a trooper in the King's service. On the other hand it can be set down with certainty that his wife Justina, poor as she was, came of noble stock. She was twenty-four when she married. It was in the evening of February 22, 1810, that she was delivered of her only son. It is said that at that hour music could be heard from her room – the sound of violins played by villagers for a wedding serenade.

One Polish village is very much like another. But the birth of Fryderyk Chopin there gives Zelazowa Wola a reflected glory that enables one to pick it out from a multitude of half-remembered names. The event took place in a little low-roomed dwelling in the shadow of the great house where the parents were employed. Their son was seven months old when Nicholas received an appointment as professor of French at the Warsaw Lyceum. Poland now was looking to Napoleon to restore her rights. The youth of the country was ardently pro-French. There was promise of better times. Nicholas saw that he had greater scope in Warsaw, and soon he obtained new appointments. His income, however, was still inadequate, for two daughters had since been added to his family. He, therefore, decided to turn his house into a boarding-school for the children of gentlefolk. With some of these his son formed friendships, with Tytus Woyciechowski, for example, and Juljan Fontana and the brothers Anton and Felix Wodzinski. These four were Fryderyk's friends for many years.

During childhood, Fryderyk was pale and delicate in appearance and girlishly sensitive. At the sound of music he would frequently burst into tears. The pianoforte-keyboard drew him like a magnet. It is to his parents' great credit that they did not attempt to oppose his temperament. Before he was seven years old they decided to place him in the hands of Adalbert Zywny. This worthy man was a Czech, a good teacher and a sound musician. The basis of his teaching was the music of Bach, and this, therefore, was the first important influence in the development of Fryderyk Chopin's mind. No less than any other great artist's childhood, Chopin's has been lovingly adorned with anecdotes. According to one story he played a Concerto at a charity concert at the age of eight. " What did the audience like best ? " his mother excitedly asked him after the concert. " My beautiful collar," said the boy. In another story, the Grand Duke Constantine's name is set like a large jewel. The great prince became interested in the boy, and at the age of ten Chopin wrote a March and dedicated it to him. The Grand Duke not only accepted the dedication but invited the young composer to play the work to him. Hearing the martial music he had inspired, the great man obeyed impulse and began to march up and down the room. He was so pleased with the music that he gave orders for its immediate orchestration. It was played by military bands but, perhaps because the instrumentation was by another hand, Chopin's name

did not appear upon the copies. The Grand Duke
was also impressed by Chopin's gift for improvising
at the pianoforte. When he was in this mood, the
boy would throw back his head and (not un-
naturally) look at the ceiling. The Grand Duke
was interested. " Why do you look there ? " he
asked. " Are the notes there ? "

Chopin, however, was neither affected nor
offensively precocious. Certainly his talent was
remarkable enough to attract the attention of
Poland's aristocracy, and he was always being
invited to play in the great houses of the land.
But music flowered in him with a natural grace.

At the age of fourteen, Fryderyk Chopin was
sent to the Lyceum at Warsaw, and Elsner, Director of the Conservatoire, became his teacher in
harmony and counterpoint. It was fortunate
that, at this important stage of his development,
Fryderyk was in the hands of so wise an instructor
as this Silesian violinist. Elsner, at this time a
man of fifty-five, was a musician of experience, and
a fertile, if unoriginal, composer. He had been
a violinist in a theatre orchestra, a theatre con-
ductor, first at Lemberg, afterwards at Warsaw,
and in 1821, when the Warsaw Conservatoire was
founded, became its Director. But he was no
Beckmesser. He regarded his pupils as indivi-
duals, not as units demonstrating a method. One
of his contemporaries paid a tribute to him for
discerning the peculiar quality of Chopin's
genius – and for allowing it room in which to develop. Many in Warsaw thought that the boy
was wasting his talents through want of discipline.
Elsner, on the other hand, saw that here was a case
where insistence upon rules would be definitely

harmful. He perceived in Chopin the first signs
of a style that was embodied in no other music.
How convinced he was of his pupil's rare quality
appears in a formal, end-of-term report : " Lessons in musical composition : Chopin, Fryderyk,
third-year student – amazing capabilities, musical
genius."

Here, then, was a Conservatoire in which
originality could flourish. Chopin worked well
there and, although he himself jested at the idea,
won prizes. His letters at this time reveal high
spirits and a mocking sense of humour. A typical
instance is found at the beginning of a letter to
his friend Jan Matuszynski : " It would never
have entered my head to suppose that such an in-
veterate paper smudger, a philologist who keeps
his nose in his Schiller, would take up his pen to
write a letter to a poor booby as slack as a wet
string ; to a person who has scarcely read a page
of Latin yet ; to a pigling who, fattening on hog-
wash, hopes to arrive at, anyway, the tenth part
of your beefiness." It is interesting, too, to read
evidence of the awakening of his critical faculty.
At the age of fifteen he wrote to another friend :
" Mr. Rembielinski has come to Warsaw from
Paris. He has been there six years and plays the
piano as I have never yet heard it played. You
can imagine what a joy that is for us who never
hear anything of real excellence here. . . . I won't
go into details about his quick, smooth, rounded
playing : I will only tell you that his left hand is as
strong as the right, which is an unusual thing to
find."

Young Chopin was, in fact, an intelligent, at-
tractive creature. As critical and observant as

most boys of his age, he was blessed, in addition,
with the gift of mimicry. In that he continued to
exercise this talent almost to the end of his life, it
can be said that he never ceased to be a child.
In later years his improvised pantomimes and
imitations were the delight of his friends. Berlioz referred to his playful humour and the result-
ing warmth of his friendships. His imitations of
the Austrian Emperor, a Polish Jew and a sentimental Englishman were much in demand.
Another was that of the pianist who by his manner suggested that he was " trying to catch
pigeons."

But already this gay, mocking spirit had its
darker side. Even in the years when his health was
" as good as a faithful dog " (as he expressed it in
a letter to his parents), Fryderyk was inclined to
fall into melancholy moods. The poetic sentiment of the Polish race was strongly marked in
him. Sometimes he played the jester, sometimes
was the day-dreamer. The latter aspect of him
can only be fully expressed by the Polish word,
zal, which can be roughly interpreted as a vague
longing for the ideal. The native poetry of
Poland reveals this state of mind in its freedom,
passion and simplicity. It was to inform the
music of Chopin with the same qualities. Peasant
music was another contributory force in the young
musician's development. The peasants of his
part of the country expressed themselves freely
in music. Their songs were inspired by the com-
monest objects, the most trivial incidents ; and
they sang without forethought, impulsively.
Attracted by their songs and dance-tunes, Fryderyk was often in the company of the country-

folk. These were the melodies that imbued his
youthful mind. When his thoughts and emotions
began to be composed, it was this folk-music that
reappeared in an idealised form.

His first published composition, however, shows
but the tentative beginnings of a style. It is a
Rondo in C minor, which he wrote at the age of
fifteen and dedicated to Mme Linde, the wife of
the rector of the Lyceum. The boy's essay came
into Schumann's hands and reminded him of
Moscheles, some of whose music, incidentally,
Fryderyk had sometimes played at public concerts. A later critic finds in the little work
reminiscences of Hummel's Rondos. But Niecks,
in his study of the composer, discerns no strongly
marked influence in Chopin's Opus 1. Certainly
it is far from being the work of a rule-driven
student – and in this fact there is an implicit tribute to the teaching of Elsner ; but it would be
mere affectation to declare that the music shows
unmistakable signs of a master's hand.

In the same year (1825) Fryderyk also composed
two Mazurkas, a Polonaise and a set of Variations
on a German air, but did not have the satisfaction of seeing these in print. Especially interesting
is the Polonaise, in which the melodic embellish-
ments are a distinct step towards the mature style.
The composition is notable, too, for its evident indebtedness to Weber, who was one of the first
composers to attract Fryderyk's serious attention.
He not only admired Weber's music but admired
it with uncommon intelligence. One of the
letters to his great friend Jan Bialoblocki contains
this reference : " There's a lot said about *Freischütz* being given in two or three weeks ; it seems

to me that it will make quite a noise in Warsaw. Apparently there will be many performances, and that is right. It certainly is much if our opera can manage to give Weber's splendid work. But considering the aim towards which Weber was striving in the *Freischütz*, his German origin, that strange romanticism, and the extremely subtle harmony (peculiarly suited to German taste), one may gather that the Warsaw public, accustomed to Rossini's light airs, is likely at first to praise it, not from conviction, but just in accordance with expert opinion, because Weber is praised everywhere." From a boy of sixteen, how enlightened is this appraisement of the music, how shrewd the criticism of the public's sheeplike ways ! Yet he was by no means pompous in giving opinions. On the contrary he was only too conscious of his lack of experience, and when, about two years later, he was honoured with an invitation to contribute an article on " Music in Poland " to *La Revue Musicale*, he declined because he felt his judgment was not yet ripe enough to justify his writing for a leading Parisian journal.

We may admire his modesty and still be at a loss to understand his refusal. For since the earliest years he had been irresistibly drawn by the music of his native land. No man had a greater love for Poland's music or understood it better. His first Polonaise was in the tradition in spite of its flashing reflections of Weber. It can even be said that it was traditional because of those reflections, for Weber himself had in his E flat Polonaise brought new life into this type of composition without sacrificing any of its inherent dignity and aristocratic ceremony. The tradition had not been long. The first Polonaises (of the latter half of the eighteenth century) were sedately melodious. With each composer who turned to this type of composition, a new element was introduced, until at length, in the hands of Mayseder (a Viennese violinist), it became merely a concert-hall piece. Weber's contribution, therefore, was important, and the line of restoration that began with him reached a culminating point in Chopin. Of the dance itself, Liszt has left the following description : " It was by this dance that the master of the house opened every ball, not with the youngest or most beautiful, but with the most honoured – often the oldest – of the ladies present. . . . After the master of the house came the most important men, some choosing their favourite ladies, some the most influential among them. The host led the ordered procession in a thousand capricious windings through all the apartments where the other guests had assembled." This element of formality is clearly perceptible in Chopin's first Polonaise ; but there is also that freedom of expression which characterises the later compositions. At no time and in no form of music could Chopin deny his self-expression. Liszt, referring to the Polonaises, makes the point very happily : " More than once, as he gazed upon the groupings of the brilliant crowd flowing past him, he became enamoured of some isolated figure and sang for her alone." In the Polonaise of his adolescence no less than in the later examples there are episodes corresponding to this figure of speech. But this is hardly surprising seeing that enamoured moods were now becoming disconcertingly frequent.

CHAPTER II

Konstancja Gladkowska – Berlin – Vienna – an offer from Prince
Radziwill – concerts in Warsaw – love-sickness – farewell to
Poland.

AFTER a few uncertain flirtations, Chopin at
length became convinced that he was in love. At
the Opera one evening, a singer in a minor rôle
attracted him by her fresh voice. The artless
singing of a young girl is sometimes an experience of rare beauty. The most rigorous training,
the most perfect technique can never quite capture
that beauty again. The experience impressed
Chopin so much that he was curious to learn who
the singer was. Her name was Konstancja
Gladkowska. She had not yet left the Conservatoire. The romantic boy was charmed by her
delightful voice, her fair hair and her shapely
mouth. He had already encouraged a sentimental
attachment to a clever young pianist called
Blahetka. But that was soon forgotten when the
new disturbance began. All the signs of an early
love-affair – the melancholy, the fever and pain
– can be read in his letters to his friends at this
period. A characteristic example is that which
he wrote to Jan Matuszynski during his travels
in the year 1830. It appears that his friend had
hinted at a change in Konstancja. Is it possible ?
Fryderyk asks. Perhaps she has been ill ? Jan
must make allowances for so sensitive a creature.
Or perhaps she has been unnerved by the insurrection of November 29 ? (On that day all Warsaw
had risen against its oppressors.) Can it be his own

fault? Heaven forbid! Jan must reassure her –
tell her that this passion will endure as long as life
itself, that even after death its ashes will strew
themselves under her feet. He must rely upon his
friend to make all this clear. It is too risky to
write to her direct. If only he could have done so,
he would not have fretted so long. But if the letter
went astray it would, perhaps, injure her reputation. Jan must be messenger. That is, if he is not
too bored by such a stupid passion.

Not the least marked characteristic of Chopin's
youth is the warmth of friendship that it kindled.
His letters to Jan Bialoblocki, Jan Matuszynski,
Wilhelm Kolberg, Tytus Woyciechowski and
others show that he confided in them with a dis-
arming frankness. Sentiments and opinions were
discussed freely and without shame. When
Chopin began to travel and was separated for
long periods from his friends, new faces and environment did but increase his longing for their
company again. He took great trouble to sustain
these friendships by means of correspondence, and
was quick to scold the others if there was any
negligence on their part. Since the age of sixteen
he had been travelling extensively. During the
holidays of 1826, he accompanied his mother and
two of his sisters to Silesia. They had gone there
for the younger sister's health. Fryderyk went on
to stay with a godmother, and during his visit was
greatly honoured by an invitation from Prince
Radziwill, who was governor of the Grand Duchy
of Posen, and related by marriage to the Prussian
royal family. The Prince, in fact, was an important person. But his importance in the present
context lies not so much in his position and power

B

as in the fact that he was an accomplished musician. He composed, played the violoncello and
had a good tenor voice. After this first visit
Fryderyk was frequently a guest at the Prince's
country house, where he composed 'cello pieces for
the Prince and made music with his family. In
1827, Fryderyk, having finished his terms at the
Lyceum, paid a visit to Danzig. (It was in this
year that he composed the Rondo in Mazurka
style which later was so much admired by
Schumann.) During the following year he was
again a guest at Prince Radziwill's forest-encircled
house and was working at his G minor Trio for
pianoforte, violin and violoncello. In September
of the same year, greatly excited, he started on a
five-day journey to Berlin by coach. His first
impressions were of a " much-too-big town " the
environs of which " on this side " were neat, clean
and circumspect without being particularly beautiful. As for the alleged beauty of the Berlin
women, he failed to see it. " They dress, that's
true, but it's pitiful to see the gorgeous rumpled
muslins on such dowdy images."

In Berlin he made a point of hearing as many
operas as possible. Among others that left an
impression were Spontini's *Ferdinand Cortez*, On-
slow's *Colporteur*, Cimarosa's *Secret Marriage* and,
of course, Weber's *Freischütz*. His greatest admiration, however, was reserved, not for an opera, but
for Handel's *Ode for St. Cecilia's Day*. This, he
confessed, came nearest to the ideal he had formed
of what great music should be. During his stay
he saw Spontini and Mendelssohn but, apparently,
it occurred to nobody to bring about a meeting,
and he was too shy to introduce himself. A visit

to Vienna during the following summer gave him
more confidence. At first he was reluctant to
make a public appearance as pianist, but every
influential person he met insisted that it would be
folly to return without giving a concert, especially
as some of his works were about to be published
in Vienna. Under the pressure of so much persuasion he finally agreed to appear before the
Viennese public. The concert took place on
August 11, 1829, at the Imperial Opera House.
Chopin's own description of the occasion gives
some idea of the conditions of concert-giving at
that time. At first the following programme was
hurriedly announced : a Beethoven Overture ;
Chopin's Variations ; singing (Miss Veltheim) ;
Chopin's Rondo in the Mazurka style ; then more
singing ; then, to fill out the evening, a short
ballet. " At rehearsal," Chopin wrote in a letter
to his family, " the orchestra accompanied so
badly that I substituted Freie Phantasie for the
Rondo. As soon as I appeared on the stage, the
bravos began ; after each variation the applause
was so loud that I couldn't hear the orchestra's
tutti. . . . The Freie Phantasie didn't go off quite so
well, but there was a lot of clapping and bravos,
and I had to come out again." Chopin's friends
had placed themselves in various parts of the
house in order to collect evidence of the audience's feelings. The eavesdropping produced
only one unfavourable remark, that of a woman
who said : " Pity the boy has so little style ! "
For the rest, they said, there was nothing but
praise and, they assured him, the cheering was
started by the audience, not by themselves. But
it was his improvisation that brought enthusiasm

to the highest point. People stood on the seats to
acclaim him. For his improvisations he took,
first, a theme from Boïeldieu's comic opera *La
Dame Blanche*, which he had heard a few nights
earlier, second, a Polish drinking-song, " which
electrified the public, for here such songs are rarely
heard."

It is interesting to learn that, in spite of this success, there was a general impression that Chopin
had played too softly " or, rather," as he himself
put it, " too delicately for people used to the piano-
pounding of the artists here. I expect to find this
reproach in the paper, especially as the editor's
daughter thumps frightfully." He regarded the
criticism, in fact, as a compliment. If they had
said that his touch was too loud, that would have
been serious. We may take the criticism which
appeared in the *Wiener Theaterzeitung* as being a
faithfully recorded impression : " His playing and
his compositions have a certain modest character
which seems to indicate that this young man's
object is not to dazzle, although his execution
surmounts all difficulties. . . . His touch is neat but
has not that brilliance displayed by our virtuosi
from the very first bars. . . . He plays very quietly,
with none of that dash and daring that generally
distinguish the artist from the amateur." Since
the advantages of mechanised music were not yet
available, we are compelled to resort to contemporary descriptions in order to form an idea
of Chopin's style of pianoforte-playing. Of the
pianists within living memory, Pachmann probably came nearest to a re-creation of that style,
even to the point of suggesting the amateur element at which the critic of the *Wiener Theater-*

zeitung hinted. Certainly the spirit of Chopin's music appeared sometimes to be mysteriously embodied in Pachmann's performances, despite the irrelevance of his running commentaries.

Before Chopin left Vienna he gave a second concert and, as on the first occasion, without a fee. At the first concert he had played on a pianoforte by Graff. Thinking that Chopin's small tone was perhaps due to the instrument, Count Lichnowski, Beethoven's friend, offered him his own pianoforte for the second concert. There were many among the nobility who were ready to befriend the young musician, and from his letters it is clear that, without becoming a snob, he was much impressed by the society in which he was moving. " To-day I met Count Lichnowski," he informed his family, " who couldn't praise me enough. Würfel took me to him. It's the same who was Beethoven's greatest friend. It's said everywhere here that the local nobility likes me. The Schwartzenbergs, the Wobrzes, etc., all speak in high terms of the delicacy and elegance of my playing ; Count Dietrichstein, who came on to the stage, is an example. Countess Lichnowska and her daughter, with whom I had tea to-day, are greatly delighted that I am to give a second concert next Tuesday. She told me, if I go to Paris by way of Vienna, not to forget to call on them, and they will give me a letter to some *comtesse* – Lichnowski's sister. They are very kind." At length he left Vienna with many affectionate farewells and requests for an early return. He travelled by coach to Prague where he met August Klengel, organist to the court of Dresden. Although he and Czerny had become friends and made music together in Vienna, Chopin had a better opinion of Klengel than of Czerny as a musician, and appears to have been impressed by the former's " Canons and Fugues in all the major and minor keys," which the worthy organist had probably written in the hope of being immortally associated with John Sebastian Bach. Klengel was kind and gave his admirer a letter of introduction to the King of Saxony's chief *Kapellmeister* in Dresden. On the way to Dresden, Chopin stopped at Teplitz and was taken by a friend to meet the illustrious Prince Clary. For this meeting he gave up a visit to the theatre. " I dressed," he told his faithful family audience, " and put on the white gloves of my second Viennese concert." Clearly, the occasion was important. At the Prince's house he found a small but distinguished company – princes, princesses, a Saxon general, an English sea-captain and several young men of fashion. With these he passed a pleasant evening during which he improvised upon a theme from Rossini's *Moses*. All were delighted, especially the Saxon general.

As a result of that evening, Chopin carried another letter of introduction with him to Dresden. Here he completed a hurried programme of sight-seeing, including the picture gallery, an exhibition of produce, the principal gardens, and, of course, the theatre, where he was fortunate enough to see Goethe's *Faust*. Together with *entr'actes* from Spohr's opera of the same name, the production occupied about five hours, and for this he waited in a queue for one hour and a half. "It's a terrible fantasy but a great one," was the postscript he hastily added to his family letter.

He arrived home on September 12. For all his impatient longing to rejoin his family, he was quickly overtaken by a desire to travel again. He was unsettled. On the one hand he was anxious not to spend the winter in Warsaw ; on the other hand there were various works, planned and partly composed, which could only be completed in the retreat of his home. But could Warsaw be a retreat with the persistence of a distraction ? Chopin's passion for Konstancja was now a recurring incident in the pattern of his life. His feelings were intensified by the silence he kept – an unbroken silence save for his letters to Tytus Wojciechowski. At length the silence trembled into music. When he could not confide his emotion to Tytus, he confided it to his piano. Out of this bitter-sweetness came the beauty of his melody. To the love he nursed for the young opera-singer we owe the Adagio of the F minor Concerto and a Waltz. The latter was written on the morning of October 3, 1829, and was sent to Tytus with a letter. " How I should like to play the Waltz to you, dearest friend," he wrote. " In the Trio the bass melody should dominate till the high E flat of the violin in the fifth measure; but I need not tell you that because you will feel it." In spite of the reference to the violin, some have identified this work as the Waltz in D flat (Opus 71, No. 2) for pianoforte. Certainly the composer's description coincides with an episode in this work, and there may have been an earlier version – perhaps for violin, violoncello and pianoforte. There are other opinions, however, that the reference is to an unpublished and unknown work. The F minor Concerto was not published

till 1836. Elsner praised the composer for his
originality in the Adagio, but Chopin himself was
not satisfied with the Finale and postponed the
completion of the work for some time.

Meanwhile he had received an invitation from
Prince Radziwill to his country house in order to
discuss the idea of joining the Prince's household
in Berlin. Chopin accepted the invitation to the
country and again was enchanted by his environment. Nevertheless he was sceptical about the
Prince's offer and the more so in face of his father's
optimism. Happy as he was in the company of
the Prince and his charming family, Chopin was
inclined to be incredulous where nobility's pro-
mises were concerned. A Polish proverb exactly
expressed his feelings on the subject : " This is not
the first gracious favour on a piebald horse that I
have seen."

During this short visit to the country, the spirits
of the love-sick youth were temporarily revived.
His melancholy was allayed by the presence of
the two young Princesses, by their kindness and
love of music. Princess Eliza was captivated by
his Polonaise in F minor which he played to her ;
and he in turn was captivated by the musical intelligence of Princess Wanda, who was two years
younger than himself and to whom he gave
pianoforte lessons. For her study he wrote a
Polonaise for pianoforte and violoncello which
was published a few years later as Opus 3. It
was intended to be nothing more than a brilliant
drawing-room piece for ladies. A composition of
this kind he could throw off without effort, but
he was still preoccupied with the Finale of his
F minor Concerto. It was not completed till the

end of the winter. Then, on March 17, 1830, he gave his first concert in Warsaw. As a tribute to his master, he prepared a programme with an Overture by Elsner at the beginning. His own newly finished Concerto was the centre-piece of the programme. To some the love-inspired Adagio of this work may prove a disappointment. Others may find in it an interesting parallel between an adolescent passion and an adolescent style. If any are disposed to find fault because they discern operatic influence here, they will do well to recall that it was an opera-singer who was in the composer's thoughts when he wrote that movement, and that it was probably with intent that he reproduced such an aria as she might have sung.

A second concert in Warsaw was given a few days later, and again the Concerto was the highlight of the programme. For both concerts the theatre was full, and the enthusiasm left no doubt that the prophet was being honoured in his own country. In one account, indeed, it was prophesied that the Poles would one day be as proud of Fryderyk Chopin as the Germans were of Mozart. The two concerts yielded a sum of about £120. The profit and the brilliant success were perhaps hardly commensurate ; yet there is no reason to believe that the financial result was unsatisfactory to a young musician at the beginning of his career and in those haphazard days of concert-giving.

But happiness still eluded him. He began to realise that his love for Konstancja was weakening his spirit. He turned night into day and day into night. His mind was clouded by a

monotonous, inconsequent dream. To carry her
letters next his heart was his only solace. Nor was
his deep affection for Tytus an unmixed blessing.
Tytus, a few years older than his friend, was less
impulsive, less demonstrative. He was a tall,
strong, reserved young man, beside whom Fryderyk's differences were accentuated, his slender
figure, deep-set eyes and fresh complexion.
Tytus's letters were also carried next his heart
and competed with the others for first place. To
show his affection, Fryderyk informed his friend
of the fact in a letter. " Although these in-
animate objects do not know each other," he
wrote, " I am sure they feel they have come from
friendly hands." Tytus was probably embarrassed by so naïve a confession.

In this unhappy state of mind, Chopin was
driven in upon himself more and more. He
found comfort in composing the music of his
imagination. The Adagio in E, written during
this period, is a deliberate evocation of romantic
tenderness, an attempt to sing his tormented mind
to sleep. For several months he continued to
resist the pull of destiny, always resorting to his
pianoforte or his compositions to dull the sense of
conflict. The visit of a famous German singer to
Warsaw provided a pleasant interlude. This was
Sontag, who came to give six concerts. It is
interesting to observe how Chopin's imagination
was kindled by fine singing, and with what good
judgment he described the performances of
singers. He was deeply impressed by Sontag's
highly cultivated singing, and, having been presented to her by Prince Radziwill, he took the
opportunity of bringing Konstancja to meet her.

In a long letter to Tytus, Chopin sets down Sontag's good qualities both as an artist and as a woman. She was wonderfully good-natured and rarely refused visitors. Chopin gives an amusing account of one of these receptions : " She was worn out by incredibly dull visitors : governors of fortresses, generals, senators and adjutants, who just sat there gaping at her and talking about the weather. She receives them all most courteously ; she is too kind-hearted for anything else ; but yesterday, before she could go to the theatre for rehearsal, she was forced to lock her door in order to put on her hat."

After this brief diversion, Chopin fell back again into melancholy and uncertainty. He was angry with himself for not being able to decide on a date for leaving Warsaw. He had a presentiment that, having left, he would never see his home again. It was at this period, when he was twenty years old, that the thought of death began to prey upon his mind. He was haunted by the fear of dying in a foreign land, and visualised a death-bed scene in a strange room with a casual doctor in attendance and his family and friends far away. Morbidly he continued to play with the idea until all desire to explore life and the world again had fled. His friends reminded him of his duty to himself. The great gifts that had been bestowed on him must not be wasted, they said. Their entreaties made him grateful. In his heart he knew the path which sooner or later he would unconditionally follow. But still he could not decisively fix the moment when the journey should begin. He arranged to give another concert in Warsaw on October 11. The occasion repre-

sented a kind of reconciliation between his contending desires, a resolving of the spiritual discord. For, in this programme, Fryderyk and
Konstancja were associated. He played his new
Concerto in E minor and the Fantasia on Polish
airs ; she, in a white dress and with roses in her
hair, sang a *cavatina* from Rossini's *Lady of the Lake*.
Her singing and her presence brought harmony to
his mind, and for once he was happy in the presence of an audience. There was understanding,
he felt, between himself and the orchestra. Soon
after this concert he made his decision. He would
leave for Vienna on November 1. On the morning of the appointed day, Elsner and other friends
assembled to conduct him on his way. They
accompanied him as far as Wola, the village outside Warsaw where formerly kings were elected.
There a banquet was held. To mark the day,
Elsner had composed a cantata, paying tribute to
his pupil and assuring him that Poland would
never forget him. His friends sang the little work
and then gave him a silver cup filled with native
soil. Tears were in his eyes when he left them.

With his departure came the end of Konstancja's
rôle in the story. Not immediately was she out of
his thoughts ; the letter to Jan Matuszynski, already noted, makes that clear. But she did not
see him again. After two years she married, and
later was overtaken by the tragedy of blindness.
Only through her voice could she then create the
semblance of light. Sometimes, by singing one of
Rossini's airs to her own accompaniment, she
strove to bring the memory of those early days to
life again.

CHAPTER III

ON the way to Austria, Chopin was joined by Tytus. They travelled together by way of Breslau, Dresden and Prague, and at the end of the month arrived at Vienna. There they were met by disappointment. Of those who had befriended Chopin during his earlier visit, some were dead, others were ill, forgetful, or on a journey. Czerny was polite enough to ask if he had worked well, but beyond that was not curious. " Once again," Chopin remarked, " he has arranged some overture or other for eight pianos and sixteen players, and is delighted ! " Tytus returned to Poland almost immediately to join the national insurrection that began on November 29. Chopin desired also to go but was dissuaded. Strong as his feelings were, his physique was not that of a fighter. After Tytus had left, however, misery and loneliness drove him to follow his friend. In a hired post-chaise he started in pursuit ; then, as darkness fell, he suddenly realised the futility of it all and told the driver to return to Vienna. There he found a letter from his father, begging him to let nothing interrupt his career. He therefore decided to stay in a country where Poles were becoming more and more unpopular. News reached him only after long delays, and in the intervals his imagination was busy creating scenes of utmost horror. Some of the letters he wrote during those troubled months betray the bitterness of his heart. This, for instance, to Matuszynski : " Such thoughts come when your old colleagues are filling my room with gaiety, and I am laughing. I laugh, and in my heart, as I write this, some horrible presentiment torments me. I keep thinking that it's a dream or hallucination, that I am with all of you, and all this is a dream. The voices I hear, to which my soul is not accustomed, make no other impression on me than the rattling of carriages in the street or any other casual noise. Your voice or that of Tytus would rouse me from this dead state of indifference. To live or die seems all one to me to-day." Only in the letters he sent to his family is there a note of cheerfulness, and this was falsely struck to give them confidence in his welfare. Far from enjoying the success he had anticipated, he was encountering difficulties at every turn. With Haslinger, the publisher, he was in sharp disagreement. Haslinger had published the Variations on " La ci darem la mano," and had placed the manuscript in the Imperial Library. The pleasure of seeing the manuscript there was Chopin's only reward. He looked for better treatment when he brought new works to the publisher, but Haslinger regarded them as trifles and was not prepared to pay anything for them. Chopin, emboldened by experience and now perhaps on the defensive in an antagonistic city, refused to allow Haslinger to publish them for nothing. But the manuscripts were in the publisher's hands and stayed there until after the composer's death. Among them were the C minor

Sonata and the Variations on a German air which lay unprinted for twenty-one years after these interviews.

At this time Chopin was lodging in a house near the Opera House. A description of the room he rented and of the kind of day he spent in Vienna is found in one of his letters. There were three windows. Opposite was his bed, on the left a sofa, on the right his " wonderful piano " ; between the windows a looking-glass, in the middle of the room a fine, round mahogany table. A man-servant, " intolerably stupid," called him early. He rose and immediately went to the piano. While he was playing, breakfast arrived. Often it was cold before the improvised *aubade* was finished. At nine o'clock a German came to give him a lesson, after which he went back to the piano. Then Hummel (the composer's son) arrived to work at his portrait ; after him came Nidecki, a fellow-countryman and one of Elsner's pupils, to study Chopin's Concerto. Such a morning as this was passed in his dressing-gown. At noon a German friend called to take him for a walk before lunch, for which he frequently went to the students' rendezvous. After lunch, falling in with the Viennese custom, he drank black coffee. Then he paid calls until nightfall. As a preparation for an evening party, " I have my hair dressed and put on evening shoes. About eleven o'clock or midnight, but never later, I come home, play, laugh, cry, read, go to bed, put the light out and always dream about some of you." This account occurs in a highly strung letter which Chopin wrote on Christmas Day, 1830, to Jan Matuszynski. In it are mingled

melancholy, apprehension and a charming affection. He enjoins his friend to visit his beloved
parents and sisters as often as possible, to fill his
place in the family. It is clear that, for all his
preoccupation with the society of Vienna, he was
lonely and homesick. German voices and in-
tonation intensified the mood by their harshness;
and when, in a restaurant, he heard a German
say, "God made a great mistake when He created
the Poles," a great fury possessed him.

Only fine music could compensate for his solitude. Of that, happily, there was an abundance.
He was invited to numerous musical parties. Dr.
Malfatti (he who had attended Beethoven) frequently invited him to hear music in his house.
One of the concerts there was an enchanting
memory. The tall windows of the music-room
were thrown open to a wonderful midsummer
night. Bright moonshine, fountains playing, the
warm air laden with the scent of an orangery,
a magical Vienna within view, music filling the
dimly lit room and stealing out to the terrace to
find another audience there – only one of Chopin's
Nocturnes was needed to complete the rapture of
such an experience. His contribution, however, was
not one of his own compositions, but an accompaniment to a vocal quartet. Of this and other
occasions he wrote delightful accounts to his family
and friends. A footnote to one of these letters is
illuminating: "Cicimara (one of the quartet of
singers) said that no one in Vienna equalled me
as an accompanist; and I thought, ' I know that
as well as you.' Hush ! "

Vienna lionised him. Even so, he was unsuc-
cessful in his search for a publisher. Nor was he

able to negotiate for a concert-hall. Managers expected him to play for nothing, and he had no intention of doing so. As for Haslinger, the publisher, he was then banking almost entirely on Hummel, one of whose Masses had just appeared. Chopin heard it rumoured that Haslinger, having paid a high price for Hummel's manuscripts, was poorly rewarded by the sale of his music and that this was the reason for his extreme caution in considering the works of other composers. The easy success of Thalberg as a pianist also added to Chopin's cup of bitterness. Not yet twenty, this pianist won a large following (feminine, for the most part) by virtue of a fluent, flashy technique. According to Chopin, Thalberg could stretch tenths as easily as he himself could manage octaves. *Pot-pourris* were his speciality and – worst evidence of all ! – he produced *fortes* and *pianos*, not by touch, but by abuse of the pedals. Lack of taste in a performer was always an offence to Chopin ; on the other hand, technical mastery impressed him, and he wrote admiringly of the violinist, Slawik, who could play ninety-six *staccato* notes in one bow-length, and of Merk, who was the first violoncellist to rouse his enthusiasm.

Disappointed by his failure to arrange a public concert, Chopin decided to continue his travels. But, being a Pole, he had difficulty in obtaining a passport, and when at last he received one, the hand of fate wrote upon it a condition : he must travel to London by way of Paris. His stay in Vienna, which ended on July 20, 1831, had been productive of a number of small compositions, and possibly the Grand Polonaise (Opus 22), and, again possibly, the beginnings of the Allegro de

c

Concert (Opus 46). He was beginning to be
aware of the nature of his creative powers ; their
development now was inevitable. On that July
day he took his place in the diligence and set out
by way of Salzburg for Munich. There he gave
a morning concert, stayed for a few weeks and
then proceeded to Stuttgart. Bad news came to
him in that town. Warsaw had been captured by
the Russians. To link one of his compositions
with that heart-breaking moment is a natural
desire ; and, if we bear in mind that it is con-
jecture, there is no harm in repeating the story
that when Chopin heard of the tragedy, his grief
led him to the piano where, in an improvising
mood, he composed the famous Étude in C minor.
Certainly this " Revolutionary " Study can be
subjected to such an interpretation without losing
any of its essential quality ; and to some it may
appear to gain by being related to such mental
torment as is revealed in a fragment of the composer's diary which was published by a Polish
university professor in 1871. This fragment is the
result of something like delirium. In the extremity of his anguish, Chopin gives reign to
imagination and sees the burning of Warsaw, his
friends killed or imprisoned, his parents starving,
his sisters violated by the brutal invaders, his
sister Emilja's grave obliterated. He hears the
clocks in the Stuttgart towers strike the hours of
the night, and each is a stroke of death. That he
should have been born into such a world of
hatred as this ! He is loath to let the nightmare go.
He hugs it to himself until, out of self-pity, tears
begin to flow. " There are no words for my
misery," he ends. " How can I bear this pain ? "

If, indeed, the diary itself is authentic – and no Polish biographer, it seems, has ever questioned it – then it is not fanciful to suppose that, having set down those last words, Chopin instinctively went to the piano and in the exhilaration of improvised music, lost the sense of pain. In the creative artist, the patriot, with his wild, aimless aspirations, was submerged. At this we need not be surprised, for the patriot was often strangely self-contradictory. Patriotism did not provoke him to cast away a diamond ring which had been given him by the Tzar ; on the contrary, it was one of his most treasured possessions. Nor did the capture of Warsaw urge him to refuse favours from the Grand Duke Constantine. Like all great artists, Chopin is seen to be compounded of contradictions when he is judged by normal human standards. Ordinary inconsistencies become reconciled on that remote plane where the artist's mind habitually dwells. This instance is but one of many complexities in Chopin's character. Just as his style was determined by the contending forces of folk-song and keyboard technique, of Italian opera and Bach, so did his nature consist of opposed characteristics – warm affection and irritability, pride and modesty, observance of conventions and a broad, sometimes coarse, humour, a deep love for his friends and exacting demands from them.

Men of action may be inclined to doubt the value of Chopin's effusive diary as evidence of his patriotism. In one sense, however, he was destined to strike a blow for Poland. For, through the medium of his music, his country has made a lasting impression upon the world. At the time when Warsaw was oppressed by Russia's power, there had escaped into Europe a messenger who soon was to proclaim his country's spirit with greater eloquence than ever physical force commanded. Before his departure from Vienna, Chopin had received a letter from Witwicki, the author. " You ought to be the creator of Polish opera, you know," wrote this earnest family friend. " I am deeply convinced that you might be and that you could become a national composer and discover an extremely rich vein of expression which would bring you no ordinary fame. But always keep nationality in view – nationality and once again nationality. . . . Just as there is a native climate, so is there a native melody. The mountains, forests, streams and plains all have a native, inward voice. I am convinced that a Slav opera, brought into being by a composer rich in emotion and ideas, will shine one day like a new sun in the world of music."

Witwicki continues by advising his friend to search for Slav folk-songs wherever he goes, to write them down and study them. Many paths of speculation run from this letter. Although Chopin did not choose the opera-house as his field of action, there is a prophetic note in this earnest exhortation. No opera by Chopin shines like a sun in our world, but, instead, a beauty of melody that is no less effulgent. Yet we may be permitted to believe that if Chopin had kept only nationality in view, that beauty would have been less comprehensive, less enduring. It is because Chopin's singing transcends the national element that it has power to enchant us so.

The result of a deliberate nationalism in music

is seen in Smetana's *Bartered Bride*. In the opera-houses of Czechoslovakia performances of the work are in the nature of a ritual, a national observance. Elsewhere the opera excited curiosity at first but has failed to find a secure place in the repertory. The reason becomes apparent when Smetana's treatment of an indigenous theme is compared with Wagner's, for example, in *The Mastersingers*. It was not within Smetana's power to spread himself beyond a provincial sphere, whereas Wagner, by sheer imaginative force, converts a theme no less provincial in essence into one of universal appeal. Presumably Witwicki would have been well pleased had Chopin written a Polish *Bartered Bride*. But Chopin was destined to proclaim his race with a more subtle and more persuasive eloquence than Smetana could command. That eloquence reaches and sustains a climax, not in an opera but in four examples of another form of dramatic narrative, the Ballade.

He did not reach this point of development, however, for four or five years. His grief at the fall of Warsaw demanded a swifter outlet than was provided by the extended form of a Ballade. Moreover, he was soon beginning his travels again. From Stuttgart he set out for Paris, where he arrived at the end of September. One of his earliest experiences there was a pro-Polish demonstration, and of this he wrote to Tytus, describing the unpleasant impression which the harsh, hysterical voices of the mob left upon him. The letter contains other interesting first impressions. This, for instance : " The French are a queer people ; as soon as evening comes you hear nothing but voices calling out the titles of new chap-

books. Sometimes you can buy three or four
sheets of rubbish for a sou, such as *L'Art de faire
les amants et de les conserver ensuite, Les Amours des
prêtres, L'Archevêque de Paris avec Madame la Duchesse
du Barry,* and a thousand other such indecencies,
sometimes very wittily written. It is really wonderful to see the methods people hit on here to
earn a few pennies." And this : " There is great
distress. The exchange is bad and you can often
meet ragged folk with important faces ; and
sometimes you can hear menacing remarks about
the stupid Philippe, who just hangs on by means
of his ministers. The lower class is thoroughly
exasperated and would be glad at any moment
to change the character of their misery. But un-
fortunately the Government has taken too many
precautions in the matter ; as soon as the smallest
street crowds collect, they are dispersed by
mounted gendarmerie." But if social conditions
in Paris were uncertain, the arts were flourishing
there at the time of Chopin's arrival. In literature, the first young leaves of French Romanticism had been appearing in the works of Chateaubriand ; and now the air was filled with the
sound of its rustling foliage. Chateaubriand,
Lamartine, Victor Hugo, Musset, Vigny, George
Sand – the very names echo its music ! " Eighteen
thirty-one " not only marks a great activity in this
movement but also a coincidence in the story of
Chopin's life, for in that year, when he came to
Paris, George Sand also began to settle there,
and was contributing her first articles to *Figaro*
and the *Revue de Paris.* Before the year was out,
she had published her first novel, *Rose et Blanche.*
Drama and painting were also remarkably

fruitful at this period, and if the achievements varied greatly in inspiration and competence, they had a common denominator of style and content. Whether in Delacroix or Dubufe, Dumas or Duvert, the spirit of an age could be discerned at work. The manner and mode of the eighteenth century were giving place to those of the nineteenth. As for music, Chopin had come to a city where the finest singers were to be found as well as a legion of pianists. Of the latter Chopin admired Kalkbrenner most of all. He wrote of his serene manner, his enchanting touch, the incomparable smoothness of his playing and the mastery that was evident in every note, and described him as a giant. Czerny was not in the same class. Kalkbrenner invited Chopin to play to him, and at the end delighted the young man by asking him if he had ever studied with Field. That Chopin regarded this as a great compliment is an interesting sidelight on his regard for the Irish composer whose Nocturnes were prominent among the various influences that helped to form his own style. Chopin was yet more pleased when Kalkbrenner began to play to him. He was faintly encouraged when the pianist, faltering for a moment, broke off and started again. Even this master was not infallible. After that, Chopin was not long in recognising a superb technique. He had never dreamed of such playing. The result of this and subsequent meetings was Kalkbrenner's suggestion that Chopin should study with him for three years, with the assurance that under his guidance Chopin too would become a great master. The young Pole, he said, had Cramer's style and Field's touch, but his fingering was unmethodical. This was hardly surprising, for his keyboard studies had always been devoted more to expression than to method. His father had lectured him on that very point. Chopin hesitated before he gave Kalkbrenner a decision. Perhaps he felt he had outgrown the need of a long period of rigid discipline. He consulted his family. His father's reply, advising caution, was not very helpful. But from his sister Ludwika came a letter making plain that Chopin's old master, Elsner, strongly objected to Kalkbrenner's proposal. Elsner's objection, of course, can be regarded as the jealousy of a rival teacher. On the other hand, it can also be interpreted as evidence of his steadfast belief in the rare individuality of his pupil's talent. In any case, Ludwika's letter puts many wise sayings into his mouth and there is no reason to suppose that she invented them. According to her letter, Elsner feared that Chopin would be turned into a mere imitation of Kalkbrenner. He preferred Chopin to go his own way, to be guided by his genius. For genius he undoubtedly was, in Elsner's opinion. He had drawn from his native soil a characteristic rhythm and a nobility of utterance that must be allowed to develop naturally. His rôle must be that of composer rather than executant. Elsner already saw him taking his place between Rossini and Mozart. It was his opinion (as well as Witwicki's) that opera should be Chopin's ultimate goal.

During December of 1831, Chopin wrote to his old master a long letter which reveals how essentially humble-minded he was, and incidentally, how discouraged. Although he fully appreciated the value of Elsner's advice that he should regard himself primarily as a composer, he was too conscious of his lack of knowledge to entertain any exaggerated notions of his creative powers. " To be a great composer," he writes, " one must have enormous knowledge, which, as you have taught me, involves not only listening to the works of others, but still more listening to one's own." He thinks it is wiser to put off those higher artistic hopes for a time and clear a path for himself as a pianist. To give Elsner an idea of the hopeless outlook for an unknown composer in Paris, he tells him that numbers of talented young pupils at the Conservatoire are waiting with folded hands for the performance of their operas, symphonies and cantatas, works which only Cherubini and Lesueur have seen in manuscript. In the minor theatres it is equally difficult to secure a footing, and even if you succeed in obtaining an entrance to one of them, the result is never important. Nor do composers of reputation find it less difficult. Chopin gives an example. " Meyerbeer, who has had a reputation as an opera composer for ten years, had waited in Paris for three years, working and spending, when (there being at last too much of Auber) he arrived at producing his *Robert le Diable*, which has caused a *furore* in Paris." Chopin assures his former teacher that he has no intention of becoming a copy of Kalkbrenner. He is resolved to create a new world for himself, to work – for three years if necessary – and arrive at a more secure position. Did not Ries find the audiences in Berlin and Frankfort more ready to acclaim him as a composer because of his estab-

lished reputation as a pianist ? And had not Spohr
long been known as a violinist before he wrote
Jessonda and *Faust*? He hopes, therefore, that
Elsner will not refuse him his blessing at the
beginning of a similar venture.

Judged according to twentieth-century conditions and standards, Chopin's argument is not
wholly convincing. Fame as a composer is by
no means easily accessible to a pianist or violinist
of renown. Indeed, it is possible that Busoni's
reputation as a great interpreter stood in the way
of a full recognition of his powers as a composer.
Even the popularity of Rachmaninov's and
Dohnanyi's compositions does not support the
contrary case ; for it can confidently be asserted
that their music would have proved equally
acceptable had the composers never appeared
upon a concert-hall platform. If it were true
that their works have attracted the public merely
because the composers are well-known execu-
tants, the comparative neglect of Paderewski's and
Kubelik's compositions would be difficult to
explain. On the whole, the public prefers the
pianist to remain a pianist, and the composer to
stay in his study. But a century ago, when Chopin
was carefully considering the path he should
take, conditions were otherwise. A composer
who did not appear in public to play his compositions was at a disadvantage. " Musician " was
a comprehensive term, and no man would profess
and call himself a musician who could not
satisfy all the implications. It was a case of
being not so much a jack-of-all-trades as master
of all the branches of a single profession.

At this time Chopin was acutely conscious of

the hopes he had raised and of the distance he had yet to travel to fulfil them. In Germany he had met no teacher with whom he could profitably study the pianoforte. A few had been aware that he still lacked something, but, although they had been honest enough to say so, they had not been able to define the nature of the deficiency. Kalkbrenner inspired Chopin with more confidence. Here was a teacher from whom he could learn, who would help him to draw near to the ideal he had set before him. That, at least, was his opinion in December 1831 ; but after taking a few lessons from Kalkbrenner, he found a reason for discontinuing them. They remained friends, however. Their mutual regard appears in the dedication of the E minor Concerto to Kalkbrenner, and in the fact that Kalkbrenner helped Chopin to arrange his first concert in Paris. This took place early in 1832, in Pleyel's Rooms at 9 Rue Cadet. A small audience, partly Polish, partly French, responded to the invitation cards, and once again the expenses exceeded the receipts. The programme included an extraordinary composition by Kalkbrenner, a March and Polonaise for two pianofortes with four other accompanying pianos. In this work the composer played on a large grand pianoforte and Chopin on a small one, while the others, playing on four large instruments, produced enough tone for a full orchestra. Chopin can hardly have been heard at his best, if at all.

Chopin's own compositions in this programme were the F minor Concerto and the Variations on " La ci darem." He did not conquer Paris at this concert ; nor did he defeat his financial anxieties. But a criticism from the learned, perceptive Fétis was at least a partial reward. The appraisement, which appeared in the *Revue musicale*, gives an interesting impression of the young composer at this stage of his development. Fétis applauded him for giving himself up to his natural impressions and so discovering what composers have for long been seeking in vain, namely, an abundance of original ideas. He complained of the unvaried conventions under which the pianoforte music of the preceding thirty years had been labouring. Chopin had overturned that tyranny. He did not go so far as to hail the young composer as a second Beethoven. Chopin had not effected an absolute revolution in pianoforte music. But he had given it a new freedom of expression. The distinguished critic noted the astonishment and pleasure which the Concerto produced in the audience, due, he thought, to the novelty of the modulations and of the melodic ideas. At the same time he considered that the modulations were sometimes excessively luxuriant, giving a semblance of improvisation. But this was a typical fault of youth, which doubtless would be overcome with greater experience. " As an executant," the critic added, " this young artist is also worthy of praise. His execution is elegant, easy and graceful, and possesses both brilliance and finish. He draws only a small volume of tone from the instrument, resembling in this respect the majority of German pianists." Even with the text of contemporary criticism before us, it requires an effort of imagination to realise the impression Chopin made upon his first audiences.

Repeatedly we find that it was his melodic and harmonic invention that left deepest impression. That is hardly to be wondered at. Even now, with all the manifold changes that have been wrought in the living body of music, these are the features that enable us to distinguish Chopin's from all other compositions of that period. Liszt was one of the first to recognise in that melody and harmony a new phase of poetic feeling. From this appreciation sprang the beginnings of their friendship.

In addition to his eulogy of the music, Liszt has left a pen portrait from which we can form an idea of Chopin's appearance at this time. In his eye, Chopin's whole person was harmonious. There was intelligence rather than dreaminess in the glance ; shrewdness, but no bitterness, in the smile. Liszt was charmed by the clear complexion, the silky fair hair, the slightly aquiline nose (" slightly " is an unnecessary qualification), and, above all, the well-bred deportment. " His manners bore such an aristocratic stamp that one instinctively treated him like a prince." Liszt completes the picture by remarking that Chopin was slight in build and not exceptionally tall, that his gestures were both frequent and graceful, and that his voice was toneless and often indistinct. A more flowery account has been left by Legouvé, who went with Berlioz to call on Chopin at his lodging in Paris. According to him, Chopin's eyes were brown and of an incomparable softness, the hair was chestnut-brown, almost as long as that of Berlioz, and falling in a wisp on to the brow. The young man he saw was pale, melancholy, elegant, and spoke with a suspicion of a foreign accent. His music and his nature were one. The peculiar tone-quality which he drew from the pianoforte was like the glance of his eye ; the poetic melancholy of his Nocturnes was of his very being ; his fastidious manner of dressing had its counterpart in the refinement of certain episodes of his music. Such was Legouvé's impression, which he amplified with this fanciful observation : " The effect which he produced upon me was, as it were, that of a natural son of Weber by a duchess." Here again Chopin's aristocratic manner is implied, and, on the whole, the remark may be accepted as a compliment to Weber.

And soon that well-bred manner was to help in carrying Chopin into the highest society. At some time during 1832 he wrote to his friend Dominik Dziewanowski, commenting in a characteristic way upon his good fortune : " I move among the best people. I sit with ambassadors, princes, ministers ; and have not even a notion how it all came about. I didn't try for it. It is a most necessary thing for me, because good taste is supposed to depend upon position in society. At once you have a bigger talent if you have been heard at the English or Austrian Embassy ; you play better if Princess Vaudemont (the last of the old Montmorency family) was your protector – I can't say is, because the good woman died a week ago." Probably his success with Paris society was indirectly due to the oppression of the Poles by Russia, for after the fall of Warsaw the presence of refugees in Paris brought Polish art into fashion. But his entry into that world Chopin owed to Prince Valentin Radziwill. Their meeting in Paris, it appears, was accidental, but it had important results. Through the Prince, Chopin obtained admission to that plane of social life where an artist can accept patronage without losing caste. He took pupils and was well paid for his lessons. But the necessity of keeping up appearances prevented any great recovery from his financial embarrassment. " Do you imagine I'm making a fortune ? " he asks Dominik. " I tell you my carriage and white gloves, without which I should not appear as a gentleman, should cost me more than my lessons bring in." He had changed his address and now was living at 5 Rue de la Chaussée d'Antin. There also lived his friend Jan Matuszynski, who, after having served as a doctor in the Polish Army, had accepted an appointment as professor at the Paris School of Medicine. Jan was delighted to be with Chopin again after a separation of five years. In a letter to Chopin's brother-in-law, he tells of the reunion and describes Chopin as being the vogue in Paris. The description is confirmed by another friend, who wrote : " He is turning the heads of all the women ; the men are jealous of him. He is the rage. I have no doubt that we shall soon be wearing gloves *à la Chopin*. But he is consumed with a longing for home."

Chopin could never be perfectly happy. Even at this time when fortune began to smile upon him, he could not be free of that besetting nostalgia. He took care to surround himself with beautiful things and was fastidious in the choice of carpets, ornaments and silver for his rooms. He had a weakness for flowers and arranged for a supply in all seasons. His new women admirers never visited him without some rare bloom to place in his vase. Yet, amid all this beauty and adulation, he was filled with a continual yearning. It can be felt in many of the works of this period, the Fantasia on Polish airs, the Études dedicated to Liszt and some of the Nocturnes. It was the quality that caused Liszt to say of him that his talent belonged to the sick-room, and Auber to exclaim : " His life consists in slaying himself." There is a story that on one occasion a pupil was playing the third Étude (in E major) to Chopin, who suddenly raised his arms, clasped his hands and sighed " Oh, my country ! " The incident rings true enough to stand as a fact. His natural, deep-rooted melancholy was taking the form of an almost unbearable home-sickness during these early years of his absence. It was useless to attempt to forget himself by arranging numerous concerts, for he disliked appearing in public. He confided to Liszt that audiences embarrassed him, stifled him by their excited breathing, paralysed him by their pitiless curiosity. " But as for you," he added – is there a flicker of irony here ? – " you are intended by fate to appear in public ; for, even when you cannot woo your audience, you have the power to stun it." Among the comparatively few concerts at which Chopin appeared was one in April 1833, when he and Liszt played together. Towards the end of the year there was a concert at which these two and Hiller played in a Bach Concerto for three pianofortes. On another occasion, Chopin played at a concert organised by Berlioz in honour of Harriet Smithson, the Irish actress who had just become his wife. In view of the fact that Berlioz was capable of writ-

ing admirable criticism, it is interesting to turn
to his opinion of Chopin. " As a player and as a
composer," he wrote in the *Rénovateur*, " Chopin is
an artist apart. He has no point of resemblance
to any other musician I know. Unhappily,
there in no one but Chopin himself who can play
his music and give it that original turn, that
impromptu that is one of its principal charms.
His execution is veined with a thousand nuances
of movement of which he alone has the secret,
and which cannot be indicated. . . . The detail
in his Mazurkas is unbelievable ; then he has
found a way to make them doubly interesting by
playing them to the last degree of softness, with
superlative *piano*, the hammers touching the
strings so lightly that one is tempted to bend the
ear over the instrument as one might at a concert
of sylphs and pixies."

The paths of the Romantics were converging.
It was at this time that Chopin met another
representative of the era. (But how contrasted
were he and Berlioz !) Mendelssohn and Chopin
met in the spring of 1834, at a music festival at
Aix-la-Chapelle. Chopin and Hiller had gone
there together, and, after the meeting with
Mendelssohn, the three went on to Düsseldorf.
Chopin and Hiller had planned to go up the Rhine
to Coblenz, and Mendelssohn accompanied them
as far as Cologne. Of both pianists, Mendelssohn
formed a high opinion. Chopin, he thought, had
taken his place in the front rank as a player, and
provided as many surprises as were found under
Paganini's bow. But he had one qualification to
make, and in it can be discerned an essential
difference of outlook, one that is enlightening when

D

it is considered in relation to the music of each composer. He thought it a pity that Chopin had the Parisian mania for the tragic pose. In his opinion, Chopin exaggerated sentiment, and, as a result, time and rhythm suffered. Mendelssohn admitted that perhaps he himself went to the other extreme, so that he and Chopin were complementary. He felt himself to be a perfect pedant by the side of Chopin and Hiller ; and they beside him were like " modish young exquisites."

There is a grain of truth in this observation, but, of course, it also reveals an imperfect understanding of Chopin's nature. Mendelssohn disliked the *rubato* in Chopin's music and playing because he did not share (and failed to perceive) the emotional stress from which it sprang. Even in the Mazurkas, which might reasonably be expected to have an air of formality, these disconcerting bursts of passion are encountered. The dance itself is a complex and lengthy ritual. First, the couples join hands and move round in a circle ; then the ring is broken and the first couple leads a procession past the onlookers ; after that, each couple in turn executes a dance in which an eager courtship is mimed, and at length, perhaps after an hour or more, the ring is reformed. The dance is then rounded off, frequently by a chorus. Both the delight and the sadness of love are expressed in the Mazurka, and while each couple is dancing, the others are engaged in conversation and intrigues. The dancing couple and the accompanying romances in the background – both elements are found in Chopin's Mazurkas. The dance is in three-four time, rather slow and frequently is based upon the pattern of

a divided first beat and an accented second beat.
While conforming to its characteristic pace and
rhythm, Chopin lifts the dance into an atmosphere of romantic dreaming, so that the music is
not merely an accompaniment to the movement
but an expression of its underlying emotions.
Clearly the peasant tunes which he heard in
childhood are the basis of his inspiration, but into
these he has instilled a poetry of melody and
harmony that has completely transformed them.

In the same way Chopin made the Nocturne
peculiarly his. The type originated in the seren-
ades which were written for wind instruments or
for strings. The pianoforte can hardly be regarded as a portable instrument, but in John
Field's opinion this was no reason why music in
the manner of a serenade should not be written
for that instrument. Accordingly he wrote pianoforte pieces of that kind, dreamy, song-like and of
flexible form, and called them Nocturnes. Chopin
found the type compatible with that mood which
so often descended upon him – a mood that cannot
be better expressed than in Antonio's confession
to his two friends :

> *In sooth, I know not why I am so sad :*
> *It wearies me : you say it wearies you ;*
> *But how I caught it, found it, or came by it,*
> *What stuff 'tis made of, whereof it is born,*
> *I am to learn.*

Those words are nearer the truth than Mendelssohn's idea of Chopin as a " modish young exquisite." But, greatly as they advanced the composer's fame, the Nocturnes are far from being
wholly representative of his genius. The sweet and

sensuous languor of this music has led to the
assumption that the composer was for ever preoccupied with voluptuous thoughts. In point of
fact the Nocturnes, for all their unmistakable
origin, are less remarkable in achievement than
the Études. In these Chopin deliberately set out
to realise his own style, and few have denied that
they are to be numbered among his finest accom-
plishments. They were written with special
problems of technique in mind, and with the
intent of exploring all possible avenues of harmonic effect ; yet art is in each of them so cun-
ningly concealed that it can be said to derive
beauty from the very nature of its problem. And
what a wealth of expression is here ! The heroic
energy of the first, the sorrowful tone of the
sixth, the graceful ease of the eighth, the rage and
despair of the twelfth, the joyful air of the seventh
– these with the various moods of the rest cover
in miniature a truly symphonic range. And, in
addition, there is the lyrical inspiration of the
third Étude, which, in the composer's opinion,
was the finest of all his melodies. The Nocturnes,
although they are no less various in design, are
more closely related in temperament. The
imaginative flights of these, free and uncommon
as they are, are tethered to a comparatively
restricted area. So far from being typical of
Chopin, they afford but a single aspect of his
many-sided nature. The point is worth making
here, for the misconception is still widely preva-
lent.

John Field's influence in connection with the
Nocturnes has already been noted. (Incidentally,
it has given a prominence to the least of his com-

positions, while the three Sonatas, the seven Concertos and the Pianoforte Quintet have fallen into obscurity.) On Chopin's pianoforte-playing his influence was hardly less extensive. An equable touch, a beautiful *legato*, supple wrists, a singing tone and a most delicately shaded expression have come down to us as the distinguishing features of Field's performances. They provided Chopin with just such an example as he desired, and, if some of these qualities were already his by nature, there can be no doubt that he profited by a close observation of Clementi's best pupil. A letter to Dziewanowski reveals Chopin's pride in being associated with Field, and, incidentally, his essential modesty. " Pupils of the Conservatoire," he informs his friend, " finished artists, in fact, take lessons from me and couple my name with that of Field. In short, if I were still stupider than I am, I should think myself at the apex of my career. Yet I know how much I still lack to reach perfection. I see it the more clearly now that I live only among first-rank artists and know what each one of them lacks." Nor was his head turned by success with the publishers. This letter was written at some time during 1832, and, between that year and 1834, Chopin was able to place all his works from Opus 6 to Opus 19. Some of these were published in Leipzig by Probst Kistner, others in France by Schlesinger, and some both in France and Germany. In 1833 Breitkopf and Härtel published the *Variations brillantes* on Hérold's *Rondeau favori*. There is little by which Chopin can be recognised in this work. Indeed it is merely one more example of the detested *air varié* which was so assiduously cultivated at the beginning of the nineteenth century, and so feelingly deplored by Fétis in his articles. But this fall from grace can be easily discounted in the survey of a period which produced, among other works, the twelve Études (Opus 10), the three Nocturnes (Opus 15), the four Mazurkas (Opus 17) and the E flat Waltz (Opus 18).

The last of these compositions serves as a link with a new phase of Chopin's life, in which a half-forgotten theme of the earlier years is resumed and developed. Three brothers, Wodzinski by name, had been among his friends at his father's boarding-school. When Chopin had gone to stay with these boys, he had met their young sister, Marja, who was studying music. Chopin had been interested in her, and together they had played pianoforte duets. But childhood was now left far behind and Chopin had not seen her since. During the summer of 1834, he received an invitation from Marja's mother to stay with them at Geneva where the family had settled. But he was just back from his Rhine holiday and funds were low. Meanwhile, Marja, to show that she had not neglected her musical studies, sent him one of her compositions, a theme with variations. The theme pleased him so well that he used it for an improvisation. Later he returned the compliment by sending Marja his newly published Waltz in E flat, and it was the publisher's payment for this that enabled him to take another journey and renew acquaintance with the Wodzinskis.

CHAPTER IV

Chopin with his parents at Carlsbad – Marja Wodzinska –
  Chopin meets Schumann – " the dusk " – Marja breaks the
  news – Chopin's health – killing time in London.

A BRIEF moment of intense happiness served as
prelude to this new episode. In the summer of
1835, Chopin's parents went to Carlsbad to take
the waters. Fryderyk planned to pay them a sur-
prise visit. At four o'clock one August morning,
before his parents were yet up, a messenger came
with the glad news that Fryderyk was in Carlsbad
and had been looking for them all the previous
day. His father was soon dressed and went with
the messenger to wake him. They met and wept
for joy. They did nothing but embrace. Fryderyk
reluctantly admitted that his parents had visibly
grown older, but otherwise they were the same
dear ones of his childhood. And he became a child
again, teasing and mimicking in the old high-
spirited way. " We are happier than we can describe," he wrote in a note to his sisters. " We walk.
I take my Lady Mother on my arm. We talk
about you. We imitate naughty nephews. We
tell how often we have thought about each other.
. . . Forgive me that I can't collect my thoughts
and write about anything else but that we are
happy at this minute, that I had only hope and
now have the realisation and am happy, happy,
happy." His parents, for their part, were deeply
touched by the pains he took to visit them. Did
he not leave much work and many engagements in
Paris in order to join them ? Did he not spend

several nights trying to arrive before them ? Ah !
for all their fears their loved one had not changed.
Fame had not snatched him from them. He
moved in a larger world but still was the devoted
boy they had known. How dearly they loved
him !

But soon came the parting. Chopin received
another invitation from the Wodzinskis, who were
now at Dresden. He arrived, filled with curiosity,
especially at the thought of seeing Marja again.
Adolescent transformation in a girl is so mysteriously delicate that at nineteen she can only be
said to have been born anew. Chopin wondered
how this nineteen-year-old girl would appear to
him after so long a separation. There are various
descriptions of her : some found her plain, others
beautiful. Her Italian blood appeared in the
dark hair, the fine eyes, the full lips and lively
disposition. The conflict of opinion as to her looks
is probably due to the contrast of Slav and Latin
features in her make-up. Prince Louis Napoleon,
who liked to hear her play the piano, called her
" the brunette daughter of Euterpe." Plain or
beautiful, it is certain that, with her little talents
for playing, singing, composing, painting and
embroidery, her temperament and abundant
charm, she had already made many conquests.
With Dresden as the background, the stage was set
for yet another. In the renewed anguish of home-
sickness, Chopin needed the sympathy of friendship. He found it in Marja's companionship. In
the mornings they went out for expeditions to the
woods, to the museums, or along the riverside, and
never before had Dresden seemed so lovely. They
paid a visit to one of Marja's uncles, Palatin

Wodzinski. He had presided in the Polish Senate immediately before the fall of Warsaw, and now was living here as an impoverished exile. The old man, with his white wig, short figure and aristocratic bearing, was somebody to be reckoned with. He had been a soldier, had received Napoleon at Wilna and had been taken prisoner at Leipzig. But this man, who was so fit for stratagems, had no music in his soul, and when his niece and her musical friend came to his house and played the piano, no spell worked upon his senses but a cantankerous envy of their happiness. He had been a man of deeds and had no sympathy with dreamers. Surely Marja – and he would cough noisily to let her know that her whisperings in the corner had annoyed him – could find somebody better than a wretched musician without a sign of a future. But Marja's mother laughed at his grumpiness and persisted in regarding the affair with a fond indulgent eye. For a few weeks Fryderyk basked in the warmth of a new experience. Then, as autumn approached, he prepared to leave. The morning when he went to bid Marja farewell became a memory for each of them. The rose she gave him was a symbol of his sadness, and he kept it with her letters. To her he gave a flower of his own creation, the Waltz in A flat, and, perhaps because it was so intimately precious, refrained from publishing it. (After the composer's death, Fontana published the work as Opus 69, No. 1.)

Chopin returned by way of Leipzig. There he met Mendelssohn, who took him to call on Wieck. The visit is noteworthy, for it brought together three of the outstanding composers of the time.

When they called at the little house, they found not only Wieck but also his daughter, Clara, with Robert Schumann. Was ever such a high aggregate of romanticism found at one moment in one place ? The sight of Clara and Robert together, even in her father's house, could not but have intensified in Chopin the sadness of his own parting with Marja. When he returned to Paris, the memory of those Dresden days pricked him into creative activity. He began to compose freely, and at length, with the G minor Ballade, reached a point of climax. When Schumann heard this composition he gave his opinion in the form of a rather fine distinction. It was not Chopin's greatest work, he said, but the one he himself liked best.

In the four Ballades, Chopin again applies to the pianoforte a form that had sprung from another source. In origin this type of composition was an epic narrative for solo voice. The epic quality is retained in each of Chopin's Ballades, and, although the absence of words and vocal expression is in one sense a handicap, in another it is an aid to a greater freedom of imagination in the composer and also in the audience. We have no certain knowledge of the story that the G minor Ballade tells. From its period it would be convenient to assume that Marja Wodzinska was the informing theme, or else some tale that Chopin had in his mind associated with her. On the other hand, the interpretation of one renowned pianist[1] (and, doubtless, of some of his pupils) is derived from the hypothesis that the work was inspired by the epic poem " Konrad Wallenrod," a tale of

---

[1] Cortot.

pagan Lithuania. In it the poet relates the forcible conversion of the country to Christianity by the Knights of the Teutonic Order ; the capture of a Lithuanian boy whose parents were murdered : his baptism and upbringing as a German Christian ; his plan for vengeance ; his brave deeds in the Spanish war against the Moors ; his return to Lithuania ; his feigned Christianity ; his election as Magister of the Order, and, finally, the act of revenge by which he brings the Knights into disgrace. Only part of the poem is in ballad form, and here the motive is reinforced by the tale of a Moorish chieftain who surrenders to the Spaniards, announces his conversion to Christianity, embraces the Spanish leaders and then, showing his face, informs them he has given them the plague.

But whether the First Ballade was inspired by this story or by that other plague which the composer had taken to himself, each listener must decide for himself. If we judge only from the correspondence between Chopin and Marja, we shall find little that could give rise to so intensely dramatic, so magnificent an outburst. Beside the Ballade, the letters are pale, perfunctory things. Marja, for all her temperament, appears to have been a poor letter-writer, even if allowance is made for the necessity of keeping the affair secret and the consequent cramping of her style. The most expansive of her existing letters to Chopin is that which he received just after his return to Paris. On the day he left them, she laments, the family went about with tears in their eyes. Her mother wept, referring to him as her fourth son. Her father laughed at them all but was not far from tears himself. The singing-master arrived, but the lesson was a fiasco. One of her brothers asked to hear the Waltz Chopin had left with them, and she found great pleasure in playing it, for it brought back to them the brother who had gone. The remaining letters and postscripts added to her mother's letters were of a commonplace order. A pair of slippers, an extracted tooth, a scrap-book – such items as these form the greater part of their substance. Occasionally there occurs a cryptic reference to "the dusk." A secret lay behind the phrase. After a period of economy and comparative concentration, Chopin, having refused an invitation from Mendelssohn and another from Schumann, set out to join the Wodzinski family at Marienbad. That was in July 1836. During that summer he became again a son and a brother to them, entertained them with stories of Paris, amused them with imitations, enchanted them with music. Towards the end of August they all went back to Dresden and there stayed for two weeks. Two days before he was due to leave them Chopin asked Marja to be his wife, and she consented. Because the incident had occurred at the most conventional time of twilight, they agreed that it should be known as "the dusk." And since Mme Wodzinska, in giving her consent, made secrecy a condition, the description became even more appropriate. There was Marja's father to consider. He with his family pride would be difficult to persuade, and Fryderyk's health was an added problem. When he left them Chopin felt that already the consummation of his happiness had passed. But Mme Wodzinska continued to hold the reins, and, without giving him any defi-

nite encouragement, contrived to sustain his
interest in her daughter. Her carefully worded
letters and his replies were equally guarded.
From time to time he sent her news of her son
Anton, who was in Paris, and was dutiful in
giving her information of a general nature ; he
collected autographs for her and helped her to
choose a piano. But through all this correspondence there are signs that Chopin was ill at
ease and only too ready to resort to small talk.
From the beginning of 1837 (it is clear) the
Wodzinskas were doing their best to make a
graceful retreat. In one letter, Marja could think
of nothing to say except that it was thawing ; in
another, sent to acknowledge an album he had
sent her and the melodies he had written upon its
pages, she was so formal and brief that he could
not fail to realise its significance. She assured him
of the life-long devotion of her whole family to
him, and particularly of his " naughtiest pupil and
childhood friend." The assurance was no more
than an awkward apology, a not too gentle breaking of the news. It is not for us to take sides in this
uphappy affair, but it is difficult to think well of
Marja Wodzinska. If not entirely heartless, she
was clumsy in her management of a delicate
situation. For all her sentiment and pretty compliments, she did not know the worth of the man
who loved her.

Chopin was at last resigned to his unhappiness.
He suffered in silence and his health became
worse. Camille Pleyel sought to distract him by
taking him to London for a few days. Having
arrived, he was anxious not to appear in public,
but yielded to pressure to the extent of playing

under an assumed name at Broadwood's. The
attempt to hide his identity failed. In a letter to
Hiller a few weeks later, Mendelssohn wrote :
" It is said that Chopin came here suddenly but
paid no visits. One day he played magnificently
at Broadwood's, then fled. It appears he is very
ill." The purpose of the visit was defeated, for at
this time the horror of tuberculosis made its
dread appearance. Chopin's first plan, of
travelling from London through Holland to
Germany, was abandoned, and in August he was
back in Paris. On the 14th he wrote to Mme
Wodzinska, but, apart from telling her that he had
been killing time in London, made no reference
to his extremity there. He was more concerned
about Anton (who had been wounded in a
skirmish), and begged her and Marja to write to
the boy more often. The notes that Marja had
sent to himself, Chopin put into an envelope
together with the Dresden rose, and tied the
packet with a ribbon. They were found, years
later, with a superscription in Polish, *moïa biéda*,
" my sorrow." We, too, can now take leave of
her, after remarking that in 1841 she married
Count Joseph Skarbek ; that she was unhappy
and seven years later was separated from him ;
that she afterwards became Mme Orpiszewska;
that she had a son who died at the age of four ;
that she reached extreme old age and all but
outlived the century.

CHAPTER V

George Sand – Balzac's impression of Sand – Heine's tribute to
Chopin – Majorca – Valdemosa – illness and disillusion –
flight to Marseilles.

In following the years of any man's life, there is
always an inclination to speculate as to the course
it would have taken had this or that imminent
force become predominant. In the case of Chopin
and Marja Wodzinska, the speculation would be
singularly idle, for, as we have seen, Chopin had
the germ of unhappiness in his very nature, and
whatever had befallen him in this imperfect
world would have turned to grief. His was the
genius of sorrow. There is little comfort in allowing the imagination sweetly to marry him to
Marja, for that would have been nearly as great
a tragedy as the broken engagement. Only one
excuse can be found for taking this small and
temporary liberty : the thought that the marriage would perhaps have saved him from the
unequal encounter that followed. Even this is uncertain. For there is really no reason to suppose
that George Sand would have allowed the idea of
a wife to prevent her taking full possession of
Chopin. Strong and manly as her intellectual
principles were, she was yet woman enough to
press " I think not " into the service of " I want."
She could equivocate with all the show of pro-
bity (and perhaps be convinced that it was more
than a show) while in the midst of a complex
feminine strategy. In her favour can perhaps be
cited the letter to Wojciech Grzymala, the

journalist and intimate friend of Chopin. Here she debates at great length the triangular question of Marja, Chopin and herself. Apparently she is unaware of the broken engagement. " I do not want to play the part of a bad angel," she writes. "I am not Meyerbeer's 'Bertrand' and I shall not struggle against the friend of his childhood if she is a good and pure Alice. If I had known that there was a tie in our child's life, a sentiment in possession of his soul, I should never have bent over a perfume reserved for another altar. Similarly, he no doubt would have avoided my first kiss if he had known that I was, so to speak, married. We did not deceive each other ; we yielded as it were to a passing wind which carried us both away to other regions for a few moments." For her own part, she has no wish to yield to passion, although in her heart of hearts there is a fire that is not yet quenched. But her children will give her strength to resist any contrary force. Then, again, there is Mallefille, her own lover, the only man who, having been with her for a year, has never for a single minute made her suffer by his fault. " He is soft wax on which I have put my seal. When I wish to change the imprint, with some precaution and patience I shall succeed. But it cannot be done to-day, and his happiness is sacred to me." That is the situation. Her task is set. Two ways are open : either she must avoid Chopin as much as possible, or she must draw close to him, if she can do this without compromising the position of Mallefille. Will Grzymala tell her if the other woman is fit to give Chopin true happiness, to care for him, arrange, regularise and calm his life ? She believes that

Grzymala fears marriage for his friend, does he not? – the daily bond, real life, business, domestic cares, all that seems remote from his nature and detrimental to his inspiration. " If it were left to me, I should so arrange our poem that I should know nothing, absolutely nothing of his *positive* life, nor he of mine, and that he should follow all his own ideas, religious, social, poetic, artistic, without question from me, and vice versa, but that always, in whatever place or at whatever moment of our lives we might meet, our souls should be at their apogee of happiness and goodness. Because, I am sure, one is better when one loves with a heavenly love, and, far from committing a sin, one comes near to God, the fountainhead of this love."

There is much in this long, stormy introspection to show that George Sand was striving to be absolutely honest with herself. But she could or would not see that this involved searching for motives was merely a roundabout way of justifying her desires. She had decency but no sense of morality. She was fully aware of her obligations to Mallefille, yet had no hesitation in preparing the way for his successor. Chopin was six years younger than herself, but he looked still younger, and she regarded him as a child. She was maternal as well as voluptuous, and so could easily believe that by gratifying herself she was also benefiting him.

We have already noted her arrival in Paris. She had then confessed that her one object was to live fully, intoxicatingly. She would take as much of love and fame as she could find. One of her ancestors was the Maréchal de Saxe ; her mother

E

was " a daughter of the people." A rich mixture of
blood ran in her veins. Jules Sandeau had
provided her with her first love-affair and her
pen name. She met Prosper Mérimée, who, she
said, failed to love her only because he did not
understand her. Where was the man who could
master her ? She looked for him in vain. It was
her " search for truth." Meanwhile she was
playing her part in the intellectual struggles of
the age and contributing her share to its wordy
literature. In *Lélia* she uttered her great cry of
despair, and then, soon after, tried to call back
her words. She thought she had blasphemed
Nature, perhaps even God. For He was not a
God of vengeance. He had sealed her mouth by
restoring her youthful heart and compelling her
to admit that to human beings was vouchsafed
the most sublime happiness. This did not mean
that she had been surprised by a sudden, blinding
vision ; merely that another man had come into
her life. With Alfred de Musset she set out for new
and strange adventures, and continued to revolve
her egocentric being. The break was inevitable ;
so, too, was the extravagant writing in which she
lamented it in her *Journal Intime*. Then she
thought herself in love with Michel de Bourges.
This lawyer helped her to obtain a divorce from
the boorish Casimir Dudevant, and in 1836 the
vestiges of Aurore Dudevant were swept away by
George Sand, the full-blooded, free-loving artist.
With the exception of her children, Maurice and
Solange. They adored but did not enchain her.
They even provided her with a means of liberation
in the person of their tutor, whose mistress she
became.

Balzac visited her a year or so after this and set down his impression : " I reached the Château de Nohant on Holy Saturday, about half-past seven in the evening, and I found comrade George Sand in her dressing-gown, smoking an after-dinner cigar, in front of a fire in an immense empty room. She had lovely yellow slippers ornamented with fringe, bewitching stockings and red trousers. So much for her state of mind. As to physique, she had doubled her chin like a pre-bendary. She has not a single white hair in spite of her frightful misfortunes ; her swarthy complexion has not changed ; her fine eyes are as brilliant as ever ; she has the same stupid air when she is thinking, because, as I told her after studying her, her whole countenance is in her eye." In this seclusion he listened to her raging at both marriage and love, because in each she had found nothing but disappointment. " Her right male was hard to find, that is all," he comfortably observes. " All the harder because she is not amiable, and, consequently, loving her will always be beset with difficulties. She is a bachelor, she is an artist, she is big, generous, loyal, chaste ; she has the features of a man. Ergo, she is not a woman." Balzac was a master of the art of inventory impressions. He noted many other things during this visit to George Sand ; that she was an excellent mother ; that she dressed her daughter Solange like a little boy – " and that is not right " – that she smoked inordinately : that she played the princess rather too much ; that she took fame, as he did, lightly. And he offered a criticism of her work : " She knew – and said of herself, before I told her, just what I think – that

she has neither power of conception nor the gift of
constructing plots, nor the ability to attain to the
truth, nor the art of pathos ; but that, without
knowing the French language, she has *style*."
Finally, he submits this naïve piece of reasoning :
" A woman attracts and she repels, and, since
I am very masculine, if she produces that effect
on me, she must produce it on men who are like
me. She will always be unhappy." In this
letter Balzac did not discern deeply, but he
has left a vivid surface description which will help
us at least to visualise the formidable character
who has now made her entry upon our stage.

It was Liszt who had brought her upon the
scene. He was now living with the Comtesse
d'Agoult, who had forsaken husband and
daughter for his sake. Liszt had met George
Sand through Alfred de Musset, and, knowing
that the Comtesse d'Agoult had a great admiration for George Sand, he brought the two women
together. In the autumn of 1836, all three were
staying in Paris at the Hôtel de France, Rue
Laffitte. Liszt often spoke to George Sand of
Chopin, whom he held in the highest esteem. She
became curious and expressed a wish to meet
him. One evening Chopin was surprised by a
visit from Liszt and some friends. Even if many
of its facile picturesque touches may be discounted, Liszt's description of the occasion cannot be overlooked. He paints for us a room lit by
a few candles, a Pleyel piano, ghostly furniture,
a sheet of light spreading from the piano towards
the hearth where the firelight gleamed. In this
spotlight, Heine, Meyerbeer and Hiller were revealed. Near this group was Delacroix, carried

away by Chopin's playing. In a corner, Mickiewicz, the visionary, sat brooding. A mirror
reflected the blonde hair of Liszt's adored one,
and " sunk in an armchair, with her elbows on
a console, was Mme Sand, curiously attentive
and graciously subjugated." Later, Chopin and
George Sand met again at the Hôtel de France,
where the Comtesse d'Agoult had improvised a
salon, and, if we are to believe Hiller, Chopin was
repelled by Mme Sand and could hardly believe
that she was a woman.

For the whole of the year 1837, George Sand
was at Nohant, and invited Chopin to visit her
there. Although at first he was inclined to go,
there is no direct evidence that the invitation
was ever accepted. Chopin came to London in
July, as we have noted, and then returned to
Paris. After that, his movements cannot be
determined until the beginning of the following
year when he again came to London and was
honoured by an invitation to play before the
Court. In March we find him at Rouen, where
he gave a benefit concert for a fellow-countryman.
An account appeared in the *Gazette musicale*, in
which it was remarked that Chopin's reluctance
to play in public was always overcome when it
was a question of giving help, or of patriotism.
" His success was immense ! " the writer continues. " All these exquisite melodies, these un-
speakable refinements of execution, this melancholy and passionate inspiration, all that poetry
of performance and of composition which grips
both the heart and the imagination at the same
time, affected, moved and intoxicated his five
hundred auditors." The account ends with this

extraordinary appeal : " Come now, Chopin !
Come ! Let this triumph decide you ; cease to
be selfish, give us all more of your fine talent ;
consent to be taken for what you are ; put an
end to the great controversy which divides artists,
and when people ask who is the first pianist in
Europe, Liszt or Thalberg, let everybody be in
a position to answer with those who have heard
you : it is Chopin." Allowance must be made,
no doubt, for the fact that the *Gazette musicale* was
the official journal of Chopin's publishers. But
at this time Chopin was receiving similar tributes
in other quarters where there was no particular
motive for advancing his claims save that of freely
acknowledging his qualities. In the *Dramatic
Review* of Stuttgart, for instance, there appeared
an article in which Chopin was described as
deriving his chivalrous sentiment and traditional
melancholy from Poland, his elegance and grace
from France, his deeply contemplative nature
from Germany. The author then goes on to set
down his conviction : " We must certainly grant
that Chopin has genius in the full acceptance of
the word. He is not only a virtuoso but a poet as
well ; he is able to reveal to us the poetry which
dwells in his soul ; he is a poet-musician and there
is nothing to compare to the enjoyment he affords
us when he improvises upon the piano. He is,
then, neither a Pole, a Frenchman nor a German ;
he reveals a higher origin ; he comes from the
land of Mozart, Raphael and Goethe ; his true
country is the land of poetry." This was indeed
a tribute, seeing that it came from no less a person
than Heine.

Chopin's reputation had never been higher.

His playing had never worked with greater power. Such, we may believe, was the effect of his grief over the broken engagement. Perhaps, too, it was as a result of this state of mind that the repulsion with which George Sand first filled him was gradually transformed into a tentative friendship, and the friendship into the strange attachment which so profoundly affected the life of his body and spirit. Here, however, we are in the region of speculation. No letter or document throws any light upon this period of change. Nor does Karenine, in his biography of George Sand, suggest cause or motive except to remark that Chopin's affair with Marja Wodzinska had been a poor, one-sided thing and that his encounter with a free and generous and ardent soul such as George Sand's could not but fill his being with the light and fire of a great passion. Here was one, Karenine thinks, who could help Chopin to experience real love, whose heart was as big as his own. Big and generous her heart may have been, but its first awakening seems to have been less spontaneous than deliberately contrived. The first available evidence occurs in a letter written by George Sand to Mme Marliani on May 28, 1838. It is obviously a single, detached link belonging to a chain of correspondence which, if it could be reconstructed, would help us to understand the preceding metamorphosis and preparation. Mme Marliani has been sending to George Sand letters which were either inquisitive or sympathetic or both, and of which Chopin was the main subject. Her friend is not yet ready to give her a definite answer about her own feelings. The weather is variable during the season of love, she explains. What may be in the morning an unlovely thought often has the semblance of supreme happiness before the sun is down. So she asks her friend to wait until the barometer is more steady, and tells her that, although she has no reason to reproach herself, she is not yet happy in her mind. What are we to think of a woman who protests that she has no desire to play the part of bad angel, who admits that her lover has never for a moment caused her unhappiness, who yet is already planning to take another, and finds no cause for regret, no serious fault in her behaviour ? After Chopin had first met her, he had said to Hiller : " Is she really a woman ? I could almost doubt it." We could ask the same question and, perhaps with less qualification, give a similar answer. Nevertheless, we must try to perceive in her the quality that finally made Chopin deliver himself into her hands. It was her indomitable will. Chopin's own will had never been conspicuously strong. The change that had taken place in his feelings towards her admits only one interpretation : that she had completely overpowered him. Of the tactics she employed in the contest we have no record. But we can deduce their nature from the preliminary man-œuvres in her letter to Grzymala, where she shows herself not so much a bad angel as a good, calculating general. During this long argument she deploys her forces so skilfully that, in spite of her untenable, preposterous position, she manages to excuse it without the smallest prick of con-science. She even contemplates the possibility of retaining two lovers, one to serve the body, the other to delight the soul. The question of

complete possession is to her of secondary importance. No man or woman has the right to imprison
a great artist. If ever Chopin is in danger of being
shackled, as, for example, Poland is by Russia,
then it were better to employ all the wiles of
Armida to lure him into safety. Chopin has not
yet reached her own stage of emancipation. He
blushes for his temptations and is almost piously
sensitive where " the ecstasy of love " is concerned. " This way of looking at the supreme
embrace of love," she confesses to Grzymala,
" has always been repugnant to me."

In that confession can be heard the harsh note
of exalted individualism which is so typical of
the early nineteenth-century Romantics. Their
very eloquence was intensified by the absence of
spirituality, the godless void in which it rever-
berated. In their work we find themselves continually projected as passionate beings possessed
by demons. In catching the echoes of its age,
Literature, being the more immediate art, is
always in advance of Music. The delayed
acknowledgment of Berlioz's genius has been
partly due to the fact that he was the only composer who kept pace with the literary writers of
his time. Many of them, indeed, he outpaced,
and, although this in itself does not explain the
phenomenon of his art, it helps to account for the
bewilderment and misunderstanding with which it
has always been received. In Chopin's music we
find little of the wild subjectivity of Berlioz : the
expression is tempered by a more lyrical nature.
Chopin's individualism is none the less exalted,
but its tone is less strident. Listen, for example,
to the Scherzo in B flat minor (Opus 31) of this

period. Some have found there Chopin's emotions after the break with Marja Wodzinska –
questionings, reproaches, caresses, all the signs
of love's sickness and pain. Schumann compared
it to one of Byron's poems. Niecks considered it
a composition of more than ordinary importance,
more various in its emotional incidents than the
other works bearing the same title. We can
admit both the comparison and the judgment.
Yet, with all its audacity, an underlying tenderness can always be felt. Chopin was less advanced, less defiant than Berlioz, but whereas
Berlioz was often content with stretches of exasperated prose, Chopin distilled the very essence of
poetry. When Heine wrote that Chopin's true
country was the land of poetry, his observation
was intuitive and penetrating. It was witnessed by
other publications of this period – by the twelve
Études of Opus 25 (dedicated to the Comtesse
d'Agoult), the Impromptu (Opus 29,) the four
Mazurkas (Opus 30) and the two Nocturnes
(Opus 32). Some of the Études belong to an
earlier time, but the first (suggesting a pastoral
scene) and the last (a magnificent finale) proclaim
a more mature style. At the end of 1838, Chopin
published the four Mazurkas of Opus 33 and the
three Waltzes of Opus 34. The Preludes, although
marked with an earlier opus number, did not
appear until the following autumn. They were
dedicated to Camille Pleyel, who had commis-
sioned them, paying 500 francs in advance, and
promising 1,500 francs on completion. A musical
ear and understanding will perceive in these
Preludes a reflection of those mysterious movings
of spirit that were in themselves preludes to the

alliance between Chopin and George Sand – will
perceive even more clearly, perhaps, than if more
tangible evidence were available.

Not until the end of 1838 does the course of
Chopin's life emerge again with any certainty.
Even then its motives sometimes appear only
through a haze ; and sometimes through the dark
glass of George Sand's own evidence. In her
Histoire de ma vie she offers an explanation of
Chopin's decision to accompany her to Majorca.
She had already planned to spend the winter in a
warmer climate for the sake of her delicate son,
Maurice. While she was making plans for her
departure, Chopin, whom she saw daily, repeatedly told her that, if he were in Maurice's place,
he believed he would soon be cured of his own
malady. Many of his friends thought that he was
consumptive and urged him to spend some time
in the south of Europe. During his visits to the
Wodzinskis his health had caused anxiety, but
now his case was far more serious. Rest and a
change of environment were essential. But, in
spite of his longing to be cured, it was difficult to
persuade him to leave Paris – his friends, his
doctor, his rooms, his piano. " He was the slave
of habit," George Sand wrote in later life, " and
any change, however small, was a terrible event
in his life." The fact remains that she was able
to uproot his objections, and, having agreed to
meet him at Perpignan at the end of October,
she left Paris (and the pathetic Mallefille) and
with her two children travelled leisurely, visiting
friends upon the way. Chopin made a direct
journey of four days and four nights by coach
and arrived " as fresh as a rose and as rosy as a

turnip ; in good health too, having borne his
four nights in the coach heroically." The very
words convey the expansive gesture of matronly
satisfaction as this remarkable woman takes one
more child to her bosom. In the delight of having
successfully carried out her plan, she did not stop
to remark that Chopin's rosiness was possibly a
sign of fever. When we think of the boldness of
this adventure, the secrecy of his departure from
his friends (Matuszynski, Fontana and Grzymala
alone knew that he had gone), his poor health
and the rigours of the journey, the possibility
approaches certainty. He was careful to let his
family know nothing of this decision. Fontana
had agreed to send on his letters. Pleyel's advance
payment for the Preludes was sufficient to meet
present needs.

The *Phénicien* carried this health-seeking quartet
to Barcelona on a smooth, blue sea. After a few
days of sightseeing in Barcelona they embarked
for Majorca on the *El Mallorquin*. The night
during which they crossed was so magical that
we cannot but believe that the memory of it is
enshrined in one of the Nocturnes. The warm air,
the deep darkness, the phosphorescent sea and a
subdued singing from the steersman – every incident fell into a harmony that was solace to those
two disparate souls who themselves were strug-
gling to be resolved in such a harmony. So sweet
was the concord of that night that they had no
need of sleep. All night they listened to the helms-
man, who sang " in such a soft, restrained voice
that one would have thought he was afraid of
waking the men of the watch, or else that he was
half-asleep himself. We never tired of listening

to him, for his song was of the strangest character. He followed a rhythm and modulations quite foreign to our usages, and seemed to let his voice wander at its own sweet will, like the smoke of the vessel, carried away and wafted on the breeze. It was a reverie rather than a song, a sort of listless meandering of the voice, in which thought had but little part, but which followed the rocking of the ship and the gentle surge of the waves, resembling a vague improvisation, yet imprisoned in a form both soft and monotonous." That is George Sand's description of the impression. In the memory of that night she has come near to reflecting the mood and nature of some of Chopin's melodies.

They landed at Palma, began to look for accommodation, but could find none. There were no hotels, no apartments. At length the owner of a country villa, called House of the Wind, took pity upon the forlorn group and agreed to let his villa to them for fifty francs a month. But they had not reckoned with the approaching rainy season. After the first deluge the house was uninhabitable. The walls were so damp that they began to swell like a sponge, and, since there was no fireplace, there was no way of resisting the cold invasion of rain. During the few fine days after their arrival, George Sand and Chopin had undertaken a long excursion to the northern coast which had overtaxed Chopin's strength. Exhaustion led to illness, and, with the coming of the rain, he grew worse. They were compelled to light fires in braziers, but the comfort they had from warmth was discounted by smoke which increased Chopin's suffering by bringing on fits of coughing. To make their plight still worse, they could get no service from the natives ; for the Majorcans regarded them with horror and feared infection. Before long the owner urged them to leave, and they departed from his House of the Wind and took one of the dwellings of the Charterhouse of Valdemosa. Two years before, the property of the religious orders had been confiscated, and this Charterhouse had been closed. George Sand and Chopin were able to rent a building consisting of three cells for thirty-five francs a year. There lived in the Charterhouse only the sacristan, a chemist, a serving-woman called Maria Antonia, in whom piety and dishonesty were reconciled, and two servant-girls. Chopin, Sand and her children occupied the three large, vaulted cells, which looked southwards on to a garden of pomegranates, lemon-trees and orange-trees. Chopin, writing to Fontana just after Christmas, asks his friend to picture this huge Carthusian monastery, stuck down between rocks and sea, and to imagine him, minus white gloves and hair-curling, as pale as ever, in a cell with such doors as Paris never had for gates. The cell was shaped like a tall coffin, with an enormous, dusty vaulting and a small window. Outside the window were fruit-trees, palms and cypresses ; opposite the window was his bed on rollers. Beside the bed was a kind of writing-table, and on it a leaden candlestick, which was a great luxury. A strange place ! " You could scream and there would still be silence." Nature was benevolent but the people were thieves, because they never saw strangers and so did not know how to fix values. Oranges could

be had for nothing, but a trouser-button cost a
fortune. As for the cost of delivering a pianoforte, that was prohibitive. For weeks Chopin
had been longing for the instrument that Pleyel
had despatched to him. Now, at last, it had
arrived at the port, but was still held up because
the custom-house was demanding a heavy payment. This privation and his illness had delayed
his promised compositions ; but, at the beginning
of 1839, Chopin wrote again to Fontana, sending
the complete set of Preludes and giving full in-
structions for the apportioning of the proceeds.
He was particularly anxious not to run into debt
and requested his friend to try to let his apartments in Paris. He soon discovered that he had
been too optimistic where publishers were concerned. He had finished a Ballade and some
Polonaises for which he expected a good price.
The publishers were not prepared to pay him so
much, and in March we find him writing to Fontana in a fury : " If they're such Jews, hold back
everything till I come. . . . We have had enough
of these fools, both you and I. I beg your pardon.
You have dragged round like a real friend, and
now you will also have my house-moving on your
shoulders. Ask Grzymala to pay the moving
expenses."

Chopin's exacting demands from his friends
become more and more apparent in the correspondence of this period. Doubtless he exploited
them almost unconsciously ; doubtless his declining health, the chaotic condition of his affairs,
and the delays and irregularities of the postal
service combined to throw his nerves into dis-
order. Even so we can but admire the devotion

and patience of his friends, of Juljan Fontana in particular, in saving him from utter ruin at a time when his own will and judgment had been overborne. Fontana was sorely tried. He was enjoined to do battle with a Jew and a publisher, which in Chopin's mind were two aspects of a single elementary force ; and from a Carthusian monastery as headquarters he received his orders for carrying on this warfare. Fontana was required to take manuscripts to Pleyel, to Probst, to Schlesinger, to bargain with each in turn until the best possible terms were secured. He must regard them as swindlers all, but if dealings with Jews could not be avoided, it was better on the whole to choose those of the orthodox persuasion. If Pleyel made the smallest difficulty, Fontana was asked to go straight to Schlesinger and offer the Ballade for publication in France and England, and the Polonaises for publication in France, England and Germany. Fontana was made to understand that Probst was last in the list. If necessary he could break negotiations with Schlesinger for Pleyel, but for Probst, no. Probst was a sly bird, was slow in paying, and, moreover, had no shop in Paris. To Fontana was entrusted a campaign of intricate tactics. The impression is that in all business with publishers and Jews, Chopin was now attempting to better his instruction.

All this resentment is foreign to the Chopin we have followed from youth up till now : it was a symptom of his illness. For a time, the arrival of his pianoforte was a full compensation for this nightmare existence, this unmonastic life in a monastery. His fevered brain found relief in the

disciplined freedom of composing music. Except
for an occasional invasion of villagers, who came
to make holiday or to have their animals blessed,
Chopin and George Sand were undisturbed by
visitors. Sometimes she went out to explore the
island, leaving him for whole days to explore the
solitude of his heart. Returning at night from one
of these excursions, she surprised him at his pianoforte. Pale and ill, he could not recognise her for
several minutes ; for he had been steeped so long
in his imagined music that the world of reality had
quite dissolved. Out of his nervous exhaustion at
this time were born some of his loveliest fantasies.
George Sand has described the circumstances in
which one of the Preludes was composed. One
evening he was plunged into a terrible depression
by the torrential rain. George Sand and her son
had left him that day for a shopping expedition
in Palma. He had then been in good spirits.
The rain had come suddenly. Having been
deserted by their driver, Sand and her son
travelled for six hours and arrived back at night,
without shoes, worn out and miserably wet,
themselves scarcely distinguishable from the
deluge. They found Chopin frozen into a resigned despair. He was in tears over a new composition he was playing. When he saw them he
startled them with a great cry, and rose and in a
strange voice said, " Ah, I knew you were dead ! "
Later he became more tranquil, and then told
them that he had seen their death in a dream
and, still playing the piano, had believed that he
too was dead. He imagined himself drowned in
a lake, with heavy drops of icy water beating
regularly upon his chest. When George Sand

F

called his attention to the rain beating in just such a manner upon the roof and suggested that he had carried the impression into his dream, he insisted that he had not heard it. He did not want to be misunderstood as a composer who made use of auditory imitations. Being a creative artist herself, she well understood his indignant protest, and in later years set down her own interpretation : " That evening's composition was full of the raindrops sounding on the resonant roof of the monastery, but they were transposed in his imagination and in his music into tears falling from heaven on his heart." She left no evidence by which that particular Prelude could be identified, but it is commonly held that the sixth (in B minor) most readily lends itself to the interpretation, although there are advocates for the eighth and the fifteenth, for the seventeenth and, yet again, the nineteenth.

Chopin was beginning to abhor this half-existence at Valdemosa. His endurance was near to an end. They could procure decent provisions only by paying ten times over. The skimmed goat's-milk, which was specially ordered for Chopin, was always being stolen. Not even for good money could any of the peasants be persuaded to wait on the consumptive, for fear of infection. And George Sand was beginning to yearn for a change, for further " exercise of the emotions," as she expressed it. For her that singular form of activity was continually necessary. Already she began to look upon this mad adventure as a poetic interlude, a period of transition. Valdemosa ! The name was not perfect music in her ears, for it was associated with hardships

and even dangers. But with it was also associated
a time of intellectual freedom, and, above all,
a new and full experience. To Chopin the name
meant music in the most literal sense, since that
interval of pain and extremity had raised his
creative power to an incandescent glow. But
what bitterness and disillusion lurked in the soft
allurement of that word ! And it had promised
so much ! On his arrival he had written to Fontana in an ecstasy. Everything was so beautiful –
a turquoise sky, emerald mountains, a sea like
lapis lazuli, air like heaven ; hot sun all day,
everyone in summer clothing ; at night the music
of guitars and voices ; the most beautiful situation in the world, sea, mountains, palms, a
Crusaders' church, ruined mosques, aged trees,
thousand-year-old olives. "Ah, my dear, I am
coming alive a little. I am near to what is most
beautiful." Then the coming of the relentless
rain, illness and the deepening shadow of despair ;
until, at the last, what had seemed to be all glory
and freedom and delight became a dark prison.
In that cell, which he had likened to a large
coffin, the thought of death took hold upon him.
His will was crushed in the grip of its icy hand.
Howsoever he might long to escape, he had no
strength to throw off the shackles. But, just
when he appeared to surrender to his disease
and terrible isolation, he was constrained to make
a great effort, and, reinforced by George Sand's
desire for change, prepared for flight. The very
resolution raised difficulties in their path. Lug-
gage was strapped, boxes nailed up, but no
vehicle could be hired to take them to Palma.
The peasants would have no dealings with them.

With Chopin almost at his last breath, they made the journey of three leagues in a kind of wheelbarrow. At Palma, Chopin had an appalling haemorrhage. The island's only boat was setting out with a hundred pigs on board. The forlorn little group embarked on this, and Chopin was given a bunk more suitable for an animal than for a human being. No grain of pity could be found in any heart, so great was the terror this poor ghost of a man inspired. On the following day, at Barcelona, his loss of blood was even more frightening. Luckily, mercy then appeared in the person of the commandant of the French naval station, who took charge of them and conveyed them on board *Le Méléagre,* a sloop-of-war. We have reason to remember the name of the ship with gratitude, for its doctor stopped the haemorrhage and saved Chopin's life. They stayed for a week at an inn to give him time to gather strength. George Sand was impatient to turn her back upon Spain and prayed heaven that she would never see the country again. She prepared for another move after the doctor had given a good report of Chopin's condition ; but she was anxious not to let his family know of this report lest they should become alarmed at his earlier relapse. When, a few days later, they arrived at Marseilles, both Sand and Chopin began to revive at the thought of being in France once more. They were waking to the sweetness of life again. Their honeymoon had been a bad dream which they strove to put out of mind.

CHAPTER VI

AFTER the passion came a time of quiet recovery. Life was ordinary now, and, against its ordinariness, simple incidents revealed an unsuspected beauty and importance. They found comfort even in boredom. The doctor was encouraging, and, again deciding to take advantage of the south, they took rooms at the Hôtel de Beauvau. Chopin's lungs were sounded regularly, and, after being put on a diet, he progressed so far as to be able to play the pianoforte and take walks. There is a clear sign of his improvement in a letter, written on March 7, to Fontana. Here he makes so spirited a return to the battle with the publishers that it is impossible to overlook its significance after that long silence. We can imagine how his good Juljan welcomed the letter, for all that it required him to resume his duties as messenger-boy. In the midst of its liveliness, however, is a cry which is heart-rending in its utter dejection. "In the second Polonaise you have a sincere and truthful answer to your letter ; it is not my fault that I am like that fungus which looks like a mushroom but poisons those who pull it up and taste it, mistaking it for something else. I know that I have never been any use to anyone, but also not very much to myself." And to Grzymala he wrote a few weeks later : " You know, I wonder at your good-will ; but you have

in me a grateful man at heart, if not on the outside." He was, in fact, beginning to be conscious
of his great indebtedness to his friends and of his
inability to repay them, forgetting that the artist
pays his debts to each and all in the works he
creates for the world at large. He made one
gesture of gratitude in asking Fontana, Grzymala
and Matuszynski to share the furniture of his
apartments ; but in Grzymala's case the reward
was soon followed by a further request to pay for
the moving ; and, later, Matuszynski was asked to
spare what he could towards Chopin's expenses.
In one letter Chopin apologises to Fontana for not
being able to offer him some small items in the
furniture-list, " but as the proverb says, ' the
fairest maiden can give only what she has.' "

It was an apt quotation, for his illness had left
him looking like a delicate young girl. He himself remarked as much. And, living up to his
appearance, he was drinking no coffee, no wine –
only milk ; and was careful to keep warm. He
was undoubtedly making good progress, was
coughing less, and in his letters insisted that he
was by no means regarded as a consumptive.
Certainly there was reason to look for a complete recovery, especially as the restful sleep of
childhood was returning. While he was asleep
one evening, George Sand wrote to Mme Marliani a letter which draws a curtain and allows
us to look upon the womanly compassion which,
let us admit, was one of the elements of her in-
harmonious nature. " Chopin is an angel," she ex-
claimed ; " his goodness, tenderness and patience
sometimes make me anxious. I imagine that his
organisation is too delicate, too exquisite and

too perfect to live our gross, heavy, earthly life for long. At Majorca, when he was sick unto death, he made music which had the very fragrance of Paradise ; but I am so used to seeing him in heaven that I do not feel that life or death prove anything for him. He himself is hardly aware in what planet he exists. He makes no account of life as we conceive it and feel it." That other-worldliness was never more perceptible than when he was at the keyboard. One incident at this time helps us to draw near to receiving an immediate impression of his playing. The body of Adolphe Nourrit, the singer, was brought to Marseilles for burial from Naples, where, it was thought, he had committed suicide. In spite of the bishop's objections, a service was held at Notre-Dame-du-Mont, and Chopin, who had known Nourrit, consented to play the organ. It was a poor sort of instrument, and Chopin was careful to avoid the strident, reedy stops. He drew those of the quietest tone and then played Schubert's *Die Gestirne*. The church was crowded with people who had paid fifty centimes for a chair, but those who had expected Chopin to choose for the melody a solo-stop matching Nourrit's fine voice were disappointed. It was a spirit-voice they heard with shadow-music for accompaniment.

A brief interval of happiness descended upon him when he went with George Sand on an excursion to Genoa. Perhaps she had gone there in a curiosity, to revive memories of her visit with Musset a few years before. Ignorant or heedless of that earlier episode, Chopin gave himself up to the pleasure of his new-found strength and of

finding fresh beauty in the world. Together they
explored the palaces, the picture-galleries, the
terraced gardens – all the sights of Genoa – before
returning to Marseilles. Then, one May morning,
they set out for George Sand's little country-
house, the Château de Nohant, accomplishing
the journey by easy stages and sleeping at the inns
" like good bourgeois." In June we find them
established at Nohant. " Here we are, after a
week's travelling," Chopin wrote to Grzymala.
" We arrived very comfortably. The village is
beautiful : nightingales, skylarks ; you are the
only missing bird. I hope it won't be the same
way this year as two years ago. If only for a
few minutes ! Choose a moment when we are
all well and run down for a few days ; take pity
on a fellow creature. Let us just embrace you,
and in return I'll give you pills and first-class
milk. My pianoforte shall be at your service and
you shall lack nothing." They were now leading
a monotonous, peaceful life. Until five o'clock
she devoted herself to her children's lessons ; then
they took an open-air dinner ; after that, perhaps
a friend called upon them ; then, when their
visitor had gone, they dedicated the twilight-hour
to music, Chopin playing to her until sleep
reached out for him with soft, caressing hands.
Soon after the children had gone to bed his day
was ended.

During the summer and autumn of 1839, he
gave the impression that he was destined to spend
the rest of his life in a state of languid conval-
escence. At times his gaiety returned, but more
often the old melancholy overtook him and drove
him to find relief in playing or in composition. In

August he sent news to Fontana of his Sonata in
B flat minor. The reference is interesting, especially for the light it throws upon the finale, which
critics have always agreed to regard as an enigma.
" Here I am writing a Sonata in B flat minor, containing the march that you know. There is an
allegro, then a scherzo (E flat minor), the march
and a short finale, perhaps three of my pages – the
left hand in unison with the right, gossiping after
the march." He also announces a new Nocturne
in G major, as a companion piece to that in
G minor ; and four Mazurkas, one in C minor
written at Palma, and three written at Nohant
(B major, D flat major and C sharp minor).
With these he was well pleased, as ageing parents
often are with their youngest children. In his
spare moments we find him returning to his
early love among the composers, John Sebastian
Bach, and correcting the Paris edition of his
works, not only the engraver's mistakes but also
those which had been handed down by musicians
who were supposed to understand their Bach.
Without having any pretensions in the matter, he
was certain that he could back his instinctive
judgment against theirs in editing a number of
doubtful passages.

If Chopin had spare time, it is certain that
Juljan Fontana had very little as long as his
friend was absent from Paris. Now he was entrusted with a new commission. Two apartments
were required, one for Chopin and a more com-
modious one – a small house perhaps, overlooking
gardens and with three bedrooms – for George
Sand. So Juljan set out once again to look for
quiet rooms where the novelist could pour out her

latest impressions. He took care to see that there
was no neighbouring blacksmith, that the rooms
faced south, that there was a good staircase, no
smoke and no bad smells. He had been asked to
find the two apartments in a hurry and to make
certain that they were near together. The ar-
rangements were soon made ; he discovered for
his friend a small apartment of two rooms and an
entrance-hall at 5 Rue Tronchet, and for Sand
two small houses at the end of a garden at 16 Rue
Pigalle. But this was not all. There were wall-
papers to be chosen – either dark green with two
narrow stripes or a plain dove-grey paper with
shiny surface like that in Chopin's old rooms in the
Chaussée d'Antin. In case fashions had changed
during his absence, he allowed Juljan to exercise
his own taste, with one provision : the paper
must be simple and elegant, with none of those
harsh, bright colours with which shopkeepers
loved to surround themselves. He wanted his
grey curtains put in the hall, while for the drawing-room the hangings were to be red. For his
lessons he required two pianofortes, the Pleyel
grand on which his pupils played and an upright
instrument from which he taught them. There
were orders, too, for Dautremont the tailor, and
Dupont the hatter. No greater compliment
could have been paid to Juljan's taste than that
this fastidious man should have entrusted him
with directions for new clothes ; as item, a pair of
grey trousers, good cloth, dark shade, without
belt, smooth and stretchy ; item, a waistcoat, of
very fine velvet, black, not very open, with
a tiny pattern, not loud, but (like the wall-paper)
simple and elegant ; item, a hat, light, latest

fashion, but not exaggerated, according to former measurements. Finally, Juljan was asked to engage a manservant at less, if possible, than eighty francs a month, for expenses were already overwhelming.

But there was no need to worry too much over debts. He had a number of fresh manuscripts ready, and, as usual, began to cancel his indebtedness with the over-generous sums he hoped to receive. There was, for example, the second Impromptu in F sharp major, which was finished in the autumn of 1839, and, although he could not immediately decide whether it was a poor or a good work, he anticipated a reward of at least eight hundred francs. And, in any case, he was too happy at the prospect of returning to Paris to allow his financial position to become a burden. In a day or two he would be with his friends. How he longed to embrace them ! They had been so good, so thoughtful ! Yet one more commission for Juljan before their meeting : would he be so kind (who could doubt it ?) as to call at Dautremont's again to make quite sure that the trousers and waistcoat were ready so that he could change on arrival ? Did he think that his old friend had become exacting of late ? Did he ? Listen. His old friend would do him a great favour. Juljan had not altogether liked the middle section of the A major Polonaise ; although the work had been dedicated to him, he had been sincere enough to say so. Very well ; he would alter it and alter it until Juljan was quite satisfied. There ! Could a composer do more for any friend ?

During the second week of October, Chopin arrived in Paris after an all-day journey. Fontana's efforts on his behalf were in vain, for he immediately decided that the rooms in the Rue Tronchet were not near enough to the Rue Pigalle. So he gave them up to Matuszynski and went to live in one of the little houses which George Sand had taken. Chopin gave lessons until four o'clock and then usually called on Sand, who at that hour began her day. Then their friends came to visit them. Around these two moved the variegated world of literature, music, art and politics. Leroux came, and Heine, and Pauline Viardot the singer, and Delacroix, some of whose pictures were hanging on the walls ; and Chopin introduced to the circle some of his own friends, Fontana, Grzymala, Franchomme the violoncellist, and Mickiewicz the author, who had so much become the vogue as to be preferred to Byron and even to Goethe. The meetings of Chopin and Delacroix provided the commentators among these groups with abundant material for comparing and contrasting them. Delacroix, small and delicate in body, strong in will, considered Chopin a man of rare distinction and the truest artist he had ever met. Chopin, on the other hand, yielded less readily to admiration of the other's art. In music, however, their temperaments met in a reverence for Mozart, and again in a sceptical regard for Beethoven. Both the musician and the painter bore the burden of disease, both presented the exterior of a dandy and both were essentially tender-hearted.

This re-entry into Paris society began auspiciously. From King Louis-Philippe, Chopin received an invitation to play for him in his castle at Saint-Cloud. Moscheles was also invited to play ; each played his own compositions, and together they played one of Mozart's Sonatas. Great admiration was expressed and the two musicians left with souvenirs. The occasion had probably stimulated Chopin, for in the following year we find him publishing a number of works including the second Ballade, the third Scherzo and the Sonata in B flat minor, that work which offended Schumann's sense of form, and which another critic has compared to the four cantos of a poem of death. During an age in love with epigrams, it was but natural that Chopin attracted all manner of trite pronouncements, many of them too clever to be true.

But this Sonata can accommodate and, indeed, appears to invite some such conveniently quick judgment as is contained in Heine's " Chopin is the Raphael of the pianoforte," just as some of the Études, Preludes and Nocturnes bear out the parallel which Liszt discerned between the art of Chopin and that of La Fontaine.

Liszt's admiration for Chopin was always generously expressed. The fact that the two were rivals in the hectic music-world of Paris did not prevent Liszt from fully appreciating the other's qualities. In 1841 Liszt had returned to Paris and was once again the idol of feminine society and the object of hysterical adulation. But his own success did not blind him to that of another artist. After Chopin had given a concert at the Salle Pleyel (on April 26, 1841), Liszt wrote a glowing account of it in the *Gazette musicale*. First he described the scene and the audience – elegant women, fashionable young men, famous artists, financiers, noblemen, the whole *élite* of society assembling in the finely illuminated rooms and vying with one another for the seats nearest to the platform. Then he paid this tribute to Chopin : " His exquisite repute has remained untouched by any attack. Criticism has been absolutely silent before it, as if posterity were already present. And in the whole of the brilliant audience which rallied to the poet, whose silence had been too long, there was no reserve or restraint. All mouths were full of the same praise." Chopin was now at the pinnacle of his fame. He realised that he could approach the publishers again with advantage. His friend, Fontana, was pressed into service, and through him he shrewdly reopened negotiations. The C sharp minor Prelude (Opus 45) and the F sharp minor Polonaise (Opus 44) were sold and published by two houses. The Prelude reveals how chastened by experience the composer had been since he wrote the earlier Preludes ; and in the Polonaise the same sharp poignancy is felt. Liszt was deeply impressed by the latter, and, as usual, was ready with one of his " as it were " descriptions. The music suggested to him a dream told at the end of a sleepless night with a grey winter dawn drearily breaking. In the vehemence of the chief motive he discovered a sinister element such as can be felt before the breaking of a hurricane. He imagined here an exasperated cry, a challenge to all the forces of Nature, and immediately after this he heard (in the incessant recurrence of the tonic-note) the reverberations of cannon-fire. In his opinion the like of this passage was not to be found in the whole range of music. The effect of it was deepened, he thought, by the pastoral scene which came suddenly into view – " a mazurka in idyllic style which almost seems to diffuse a fragrance of mint and marjoram." The end, too, was like a dream, inconclusive, intangible, enthralling. After reading so highly imaginative an interpretation, it is interesting to learn that, of all those who played his music, Chopin preferred Liszt ; interesting, but puzzling, since it is certain that there was a wide difference between Liszt's and Chopin's own performances. The explanation probably lies in the fact that Chopin's style of playing was partly determined by physical limitations, and that he was incapable of realising at the keyboard the passionate force which had inspired some of his creative work.

But his gentle, eerie touch charmed the society of Paris. About ten months after his first concert in the Salle Pleyel he gave another, and with equal success. A Chopin concert was a grand opportunity for gossip writers, and we have plenty of evidence to show that the audience, on this as on the former occasion, was brilliance itself. Indeed we would readily exchange these dull inventories of gold ribbons, pale blue gauze, strings of quivering pearls, the freshest roses and pinks, and so forth, for one sentence that would make alive a moment of Chopin's playing. We read that George Sand was at the concert and that she attracted much attention. The programme included Chopin's latest compositions, the third Ballade, three Mazurkas, three Études, four Nocturnes, the D flat Prelude and the G flat major Impromptu, and, in addition, Mme Viardot sang and Franchomme played the violoncello.

These successes did little to weaken Chopin's rooted prejudice against playing in public. The concert of 1841 was the first he had given in Paris for nine years. That he preferred to play to an intimate gathering is confirmed by Berlioz, who wrote : " A small circle of chosen listeners, who, he believed, had a real desire to hear him, was the only thing which would persuade him to approach the piano. But then, what emotions he was able to arouse ! In what ardent and melancholy reveries he loved to pour forth his soul ! It was about midnight, as a rule, that he would abandon himself most completely. Then, in obedience to the mute prayer of some fine, speaking eyes, he became a poet." Not only in response to a yearning look did he become so, but also under the influence of a poetic mind, such as that of Mickiewicz. The description of " poet " is apt when we think of the composer of the four Ballades. M. Cortot's suggestion that these compositions were actually based on Mickiewicz's Lithuanian ballads is at least plausible. The third Ballade, which Chopin had played for the first time at that Paris concert, is, according to M. Cortot, inspired by Mickiewicz's version of the legend called " The Switez Woman." A hunter and a maiden meet in a wood, so the story goes. She, drawing from him a vow of faithfulness, accepts his love and takes her leave. He starts to walk home by the side of the haunted Switez lake, and on the water's edge sees another girl. The sight of her attracts him, and, through the marsh, he makes his way towards her, then discovers it is the first maiden, the nymph of the lake. For his fickleness she upbraids him, and, dragging him beneath the waters, drowns him. His ghost is wailing under the larches on the shore while she dances in the water. The fourth Ballade is, in M. Cortot's opinion, linked with a legend called " Trzech Budrysów." Budrys is a patriarch of pagan Lithuania. He sends his three sons out into the world to seek their fortunes. The best way, he tells them, is to join an army and benefit by plunder. Let the first follow the general who is attacking the Russians and bring back sables ; let the second join the forces against the German Knights of the Cross and bring back vestments and amber ; let the third ride to Poland and seize part of the wealth of that country in the form of a wife. It is the last of these propositions which makes the strongest appeal : the sons go forth and each returns with a Polish bride.

Even if we have no actual proof that these legends are the basic inspiration of the Ballades, it is but natural to look for some such origin. For these magnificent flights of imagination could not have started from a prosaic level ; on the other hand, if we think of them as springing from a poetic plane, their beauty of balance and move-ment becomes immediately apparent. This is true of all Chopin's compositions. No composer reveals so clearly the futility of attempting to mark a boundary-line between the regions of " programme " and of " absolute " music. Even in the works where fond commentators have dis-covered incidents of imitation (whether of bells, raindrops or cannon-fire), there is an essential element which eludes the clumsy description of programme-music. As for the Ballades, we can equivocate and say that they are both " pro-

G

gramme " and " absolute " music ; but we shall
be nearer the truth if we avoid compromise and
boldly declare that they are neither. Berlioz
gives the cue. They are poetic music. Whether
he was improvising or composing, Chopin always
became a poet.

CHAPTER VII

Chopin as teacher – George Sand's invalid – Ludwika at Nohant – Sand's children – conflict – the final break.

THIS poet, however, was not so much a dreamer that he neglected the more practical aspects of his art. As a teacher, for example, he was earnest and thorough. One of his pupils, Carl Mikuli, has left a description of Chopin's style of playing. Freedom and facility were its characteristics. The tone, especially in *cantabile* passages, was full ; only Field could be compared with him in this respect. Whenever the music called for energy he gave it, but never coarsely. In episodes of a delicate nature his touch was enchanting. Intensity and elegance were mingled in all his interpretations. Although his hand was not large, he had a wide stretch. No effort was apparent in his playing ; scale passages were executed with a marvellous smoothness.

Chopin did not regard teaching as drudgery. He devoted himself whole-heartedly to his pupils, especially in the matter of securing freedom of muscular movement. In order to do this effectively, he sought to enlist the pupil's intelligence for practising exercises, and in this was opposed to Kalkbrenner, who advised his pupils to read while they were going through their mechanical studies. Chopin required the student to play scales evenly and with full tone, beginning with those containing black notes and ending with C major. As studies, he held Clementi's " Preludes

and Exercises " in high esteem ; then he gave
his pupils the same author's " Gradus," then the
studies of Cramer and Moscheles. For the development of the interpretative sense, Chopin
chose works from Dussek, Mozart, Handel,
Beethoven, Weber, Mendelssohn, Hiller, Schumann and from Bach's " Forty-eight." No pupil
of his could overlook the importance of phrasing.
His own phrasing was founded upon the principles
of vocal style, and, except to obtain a special
effect, he was never heard to break up an episode
into short sentences. The technique which was
necessary for the singing of a Bellini aria was
equally necessary for the performance of the
pianoforte music he chose for his pupils, especially
his own compositions.

To turn for a moment to this more active side
of Chopin's life affords a welcome relief. But if
we would truly follow the course of his existence
we must walk again among the shadows. There
is a pathetic contrast between Chopin the teacher
and Chopin the regular invalid of George Sand's
establishment. After the Paris concert of 1842
the routine of life continued. The remainder of
the winter was passed in Paris ; the summer at
Nohant. During that summer Delacroix was
also a guest, and in each increased an admiration
for the other man. Delacroix wrote : " From time
to time there are wafted to you through the
window opening on the garden, bursts of Chopin's
music as he works there ; all this is mingled with
the song of nightingales and the perfume of roses."
And again : " I have endless tête-à-tête conversations with Chopin. I am very fond of him and
he is a man of rare distinction." Chopin for his

part wrote on a later occasion : " Delacroix is the most admirable artist whom one could meet ; I have spent delightful hours with him. He adores Mozart and knows all his operas by heart." Before we pass on to the last tragic years, we turn to give a grateful thought to Delacroix.

Chopin and George Sand were in Paris again in the autumn. They were living now at Nos. 5 and 9 in the Square d'Orléans. Between these apartments, at No. 7, lived Mme Marliani, and the three shared expenses. But although Chopin had a separate sitting-room where he could retire and compose, he was rarely in a creative mood. Most of his music during these years was written at Nohant.

Many uneventful months passed by. In September 1843 George Sand took her invalid for a little expedition to the banks of the Creuse. They travelled across picturesque mountains where there were neither roads nor inns. Chopin slept on straw and travelled on a donkey. George Sand's theory was that his salvation lay in taking risks and in physical fatigue. During the following spring there came a terrible blow, the news of his father's death. Two years earlier, his friend, Jan Matuszynski, had died of tuberculosis. These heavy losses had a visible effect upon him, and George Sand watched him with increasing anxiety. A crisis was averted by the arrival in France of Chopin's eldest sister, Ludwika, with her husband. There was the question of inviting them to Nohant. If Chopin had scruples, George Sand had none. She sent the invitation, and paved the way with a long explanation of Chopin's decline in health since his sister had last seen him.

In this letter the appropriating mind is immediately at work : " You will find my dear child very
sickly and changed, but do not be too much
alarmed for his health. It has been the same, with
no general alteration, for the last six years, during
which I have seen him every day. A rather
severe fit of coughing every morning, two or three
more serious attacks every winter, lasting no more
than two or three days each, a little suffering
from neuralgia from time to time, that is his
usual condition." She then expresses the hope
that he will grow stronger in time, a hope which,
in view of the symptoms she has described, appears to be ingenuously optimistic. She extends
a welcome to Ludwika and is certain that the
visit will help Chopin to make progress.

Ludwika Jendrzejewicz and her husband spent
August at Nohant. As George Sand had anticipated, the reunion with his sister had a bene-
ficent influence upon Chopin. He suffered for a
few days after her departure, but from her visit
goodness came in that it purged him of all bitterness and gave him courage to face life again.
" I assure you," George Sand wrote to Ludwika,
" you are the best doctor he has ever had." So
far from finding cause for offence in her brother's
relations with Sand, Ludwika appears to have
been a conciliatory force. Indeed, Sand decided
that Ludwika was far more progressive than her
brother, and that it was thanks to her that Chopin,
without knowing it, had discarded all his pre-
judices. George Sand wrote immediately to her
friend, Mme Marliani, to let her know of this
remarkable and unconscious conversion.

As we shall see later, the conversion was but

the prelude to a complete rupture. Meanwhile Chopin's malady continued to make its slow and deadly advance, and both he and George Sand tried to keep the secret. He did not want her to worry about his health ; she, on the other hand, managed to secure information about his condition without his knowledge and did all she could to prevent him hearing the disquieting news. He was very ill during the winter of 1845 and the following spring, but he followed his usual plans and gave a dinner-party to a few friends (including Pauline Viardot and Delacroix) before preparing for yet another summer at Nohant. When he arrived there, the house was pervaded by a strangeness. Thinking that he would defeat it so, he rearranged his furniture. But the atmosphere remained. Somehow, it was associated with an intense longing to see his sister and loved ones again. " I have always one foot with you," he wrote to Ludwika and her husband, " and the other in the room next door where my hostess works, and none at all in my own home just now, but always in imaginary places." There was, however, the silver link of music, and with delight he wrote to tell his sister that Pauline Viardot had promised to sing for her some of his favourite Spanish melodies when she came to Warsaw. Those tunes, which Pauline Viardot herself had collected, would remind Ludwika of him, just as the embroidered slipper which she had left behind at Nohant, and he had treasured ever since, made her presence real to him.

But this strangeness was not wholly accounted for by home-sickness. It was a presage of unhappiness to come. In that house where the two

artists took refuge that they might create, a contrary element was gaining ground in an unsuspected quarter. It was in the hearts of the
children there that the seeds of the final conflict
had been sown.

Maurice now had come of age, and, although he
possessed talent and intelligence, gave no promise
of definite accomplishment. His mother adored
and spoiled him, and he returned the affection.
In the past he had been quick to note her unhappy moods and as quick to ascribe them to
the petulance of her invalid. In the beginning,
Chopin and Maurice had been good friends, but
after the Majorca expedition the boy became
more and more critical and suspicious. Chopin,
we can well understand, was hardly an ideal
companion for a growing boy, even in normal
circumstances. And it would have been hardly
possible for George Sand to invent in fiction a
situation more abnormal than this which she had
created in actual life. A son, who doted on his
mother and occasionally visited his father, was
expected to live harmoniously with a sick man
and a genius who was his mother's lover – was
ever tragedy more completely conceived? That
Chopin was great and famous, did that count
for anything with an undisciplined boy? In his
eyes this genius was merely a difficult and sometimes bad-humoured man. Sooner or later
Chopin was bound to make a tactical error. No
man can escape destiny. The arrival of a new
character brought the latent antagonism to a
head. A nonentity played this important rôle in
the working-out of Chopin's destiny. George
Sand had taken pity on one of her bourgeois

relations, Augustine, the daughter of her cousin, and offered her a temporary home. Maurice had immediately taken Augustine to his heart. The girl was well liked by everybody except Solange, who almost invariably disagreed with her brother's tastes. In so far as it affected him, Chopin was inclined to side with Solange in the matter. When it was suspected that Maurice had become Augustine's lover, George Sand vehemently denied it, but Solange took care to encourage the growth of the suspicion in Chopin's mind. Solange had long been nursing grievances and was now passing through the most dangerous phase of jealousy, of which her mother was fully aware. George Sand described her nineteen-year-old daughter as beautiful, with a remarkable mind, and bewailed the fact that, whereas her upbringing should have made of her a saint or a heroine, she was essentially a child of her own century, that century which was damned. Everything was passion with her – an icy passion that was very deep, inexplicable and terrifying. Secretive and perverse, she watched the effect of her magnetic adolescence upon her mother's lover. Perchance one day, looking on that picture and then on this, he would yearn after that wild freshness of morning which her mother could never give him. At least it was pleasant to play with such thoughts. George Sand found herself in an unequal struggle with an image of her younger self. But, if her sufferings were great, Chopin's now were infinitely greater. Little misunderstandings broke like great storms over his head ; his nervousness became chronic and alarming.

During these critical months, George Sand was

publishing her *Lucrezia Floriani*. It was generally
accepted that in this book she had represented
herself in the character of Lucrezia, and Chopin
in the character of Prince Karol. Although
she herself denied that the Prince was intended
to be Chopin, it is interesting nevertheless to
note coincidences. Prince Karol is described as
being delicate both in body and mind, and as
having a charming, sexless beauty. He was
" something like those ideal creatures with which
the poetry of the Middle Ages used to adorn
Christian churches ; an angel, fair of face as a
tall, sad woman, pure and slender in form as a
young god of Olympus, and, to crown this union
of qualities, an expression at once tender and
severe, at once chaste and passionate. Nothing
could be at once purer and more elevated than
his thoughts, nothing could exceed the tenacity
and exclusiveness of his affections or his devotion
even in the smallest trifles." Lucrezia, weary
after fifteen passionate years of life, meets him.
But she has done with love ; she will care for
this young prince as his mother once cared for
him. Providence has sent her into his life. In the
past she had " protected and rehabilitated, saved
or attempted to save the men whom she had
dearly loved. Tenderly chiding their vices,
devotedly atoning for their faults, she had almost
made gods of these mere mortals. But she had
sacrificed herself too completely to succeed." As
for Prince Karol, he fails to understand her. He
dislikes her background of bohemian free-and-
easiness and certain hard and common elements
in her nature. He pains her without realising
that he can do so, persuading himself that she is

insensible, that, in spite of moments of kindness, nothing as a rule can affect a nature so strong and resisting. He appears almost to be jealous of his mistress's very health. Only when Lucrezia is so overcome as to admit her suffering, does he reveal his charm once more. At such times he adores her more than ever before. Soon, however, he becomes unbearable again, and, in the end, Lucrezia dies of the harsh treatment he metes out to her.

It is impossible to read this story without being impressed by the similarity it bears to the story of George Sand and Chopin. She was not the only author who solemnly declared that the characters in her book were not intended to represent living people, and at the same time drew them in such a manner that their origin was unmistakable. Both in her novels and in her subsequent hot denials she can be classed with all those eager writers who, having found " good copy " in their own lives, have told stories and afterwards fibbed about them. George Sand attempted to persuade her public that the book had no relation to her own life, and, in order to do so, declared that Chopin did not recognise himself in the character of Karol. A naïve piece of evidence ! George Sand's Prince is certainly a travesty of the real Chopin, but, far from proving that Chopin was out of her mind when she created the character, the differences can be used to support the opposite case.

Had Liszt been moved to create a work of fiction with Chopin as the central figure, he, perhaps, would have given us a more authentic character. From his recorded observations and comments we can guess at some of the features which Liszt would have embodied in the creation. The character would probably have been egocentric and reserved ; uninterested in other people's conversations ; a Catholic and a patriot who rarely spoke about religion or his country ; anxious to avoid new friendships and careful to protect himself by means of a pleasant manner or, if necessary, by sarcasm ; sensitive, easily hurt but entirely without resentment ; a man of whims, surprising oddities and the faults which are usually excused in artists ; a gay creature for all his secret suffering ; one for whom music was the sum of all experience, the only medium through which he could express the subtle variations of his moods.

Since music cannot be translated into hard historical facts, and since his letters to his family betray nothing of his inner suffering, we are left in ignorance of Chopin's point of view as the climax approached. And in the *Histoire de ma vie* (among the very best of her works) George Sand is reserved in her account of the actual breach. She recognised that, outside the region of the arts, she was almost wholly at variance with Chopin's tastes and opinions. His Catholicism, for instance, was in her eyes little better than superstition. She complained that, after the deaths of his great friend and his father, he derived not comfort but terror from his religion. Then he would dwell upon thoughts of his own death, and paint the scene with all the lurid, nightmare colours of the Slav legends. She was impatient with these feverish imaginings, and he, in turn, was irritated by her scornful superiority. She took pains, however, to set down that she had had no desire to dominate his personality ; also, that in his relations with her, he had been kindness and devotion personified. But between Chopin and her son the misunderstanding became more and more grievous. Sometimes, in a fit of irritability, Chopin, by a hasty word, wounded Maurice's feelings. A moment later they embraced, " but the grain of sand had fallen into the peaceful lake and one by one the pebbles began to fall into it." A letter which George Sand wrote on November 2, 1847, contains a more expansive version of the conflict than we find in her autobiography. She describes Chopin's character as becoming more and more embittered every day. He had gone so far as to inflict outbursts of vexation, temper and jealousy upon her in the presence of all her friends and her children. She continued the letter with this remarkable passage : " Maurice began to be indignant with him. Knowing and seeing the chastity of my relations, he could also see that this poor suffering spirit involuntarily, and perhaps in spite of himself, posed as a lover, as a husband, as though he had rights over my thoughts and actions. He was on the point of losing his temper, and telling him to his face that he was putting me in a ridiculous position at the age of forty-three, and abusing my kindness, patience and pity for his nervous and suffering condition." To print these sentences in italics would be an unnecessary emphasis. Their significance cannot easily be overlooked. In the next part of the letter, Sand declared that " the poor child " was not even able to observe the outward propriety of which he was a slave in normal circumstances. Men, women, old people,

children, all became objects of his wild jealousy.
Had he revealed it to her alone, she could have
borne it. But these outbursts took place before
her children, before her servants, before men who,
witnessing them, might have lost the respect to
which her age and her conduct for the last ten
years had given her a right. She could no longer
endure it.

But six months before that letter was written
neither had formed any idea of leaving the other.
Chopin's letters to his family show that he was
planning to spend the summer at Nohant as usual.
He referred to his Sonata for Violoncello and
Pianoforte, which he had just played with Franchomme, and then sent news of Solange's approaching marriage, not with a country neighbour
as it was at first rumoured, but with Clésinger
the sculptor. Chopin regretted her new choice,
and the fact was cited by George Sand as another
instance of his inability to see things fairly and
of his total misunderstanding of human nature.
Against this harsh judgment a passage in one of
Chopin's letters to his family can be set : " Mme
S. writes me that she will be here at the end of
next month and to wait for them. Probably it
is on account of Sol's wedding (but not with the
man about whom I told you). May God grant
them good things. In the last letter they were all
cheerful, so I have good hopes. If anyone deserves
happiness, it is Mme S." In addition to this
letter, there are many others (written at this time
to his family, to George Sand and to Solange) to
prove that Sand had been both hasty and clumsy
in drawing conclusions. Particularly charming is
the note which Chopin sent to Solange at the

time of her marriage : " I have already asked your mother, a few days ago, to convey to you my sincerest wishes for your future ; and now I cannot refrain from telling you of all the pleasure that I have derived from your delightful little letter, from which you appear to me to be so happy. You are at the summit of joy and I hope you will always remain there. With all my soul I desire your unchanging prosperity." The hope was vain. Soon after the marriage a terrible discord was struck, and it was not Chopin but George Sand herself who was chiefly involved.

It is not necessary here to analyse every motive and emotion which contributed to this conflict. It can be summarised thus : with Maurice's approval, Augustine became engaged to his friend, Theodore Rousseau ; Solange, hating Augustine and embittered against Maurice, informed Rousseau of the intimacy which she had suspected between the two ; the engagement was suddenly broken off ; George Sand was deeply hurt by her daughter's insinuations ; when Solange and her husband returned to Nohant there was a violent scene between the Clésingers on the one side and George and her son on the other ; Clésinger raised a hammer to strike Maurice, George, throwing herself between them, received a blow on the chest, and Maurice, armed with a pistol, was about to kill Clésinger but was prevented by a servant and some friends who had witnessed the storm. Chopin was then in Paris and Solange hastened to win him over to her side. In this she was successful, and for a time Chopin ceased to write to her mother. When at length he sent a letter she turned every word

of it against him, and laughed to scorn his digni-
fied, sermonising manner. Her answer was the
blow that made the final breach. Chopin read
it to Delacroix who could not but admit its cruelty.
That happened in July. A few weeks later George
Sand wrote, begging a friend to send her news of
Chopin's health. Only that. She was not interested in what he was thinking or feeling, and
already she had regained her magnificent im-
munity from all regret. But Chopin was still
enslaved. Liszt has borne witness to the fruitless
efforts of friends to keep the unhappy subject out
of his thoughts. Chopin believed that in breaking
this bond he had broken his life.

CHAPTER VIII

Music born of unhappiness – revolution – Chopin in England
and Scotland – Chopin's letters – in Paris again – the end.

IN the midst of this unhappiness, Chopin was still
able to find relief in improvising and creating
music. We can be thankful for his genius not
only for our own sakes but also for his. Upon
a creative mind we can look only from a distance
and see it, in its works, in moments of transfigura-
tion. The delight of an artist in a new achievement we can but dimly divine. But we know it to
be delight, and that is enough. How greatly
satisfying to Chopin must the completion of his
Barcarolle have been ! For sustained lyrical inspiration, this twofold Nocturne is among the
most remarkable of his works. Its harmony, too,
is beautifully conceived, and yet it is the fruit of
the most discordant phase of the composer's life –
a fact which sharpens the point of Ravel's remark
that the composition suggests a mysterious
apotheosis. Among the other works which appeared during the tragic years of 1846 and 1847
were the three Mazurkas of Opus 59, the Polonaise Fantaisie (Opus 61), the two Nocturnes of
Opus 62, the three Mazurkas of Opus 63 and the
three Waltzes of Opus 64. With the appearance
of the Sonata for Violoncello and Pianoforte (Opus
65), the list of compositions published in Chopin's
lifetime is closed. He composed no entire work
after the breach with George Sand.

Few composers for the pianoforte offer a wider
field of interpretation than Chopin. It may be

doubted whether any very definite boundaries could have been fixed even had he been able to complete his " Method," which, incidentally, was the only unfinished work he allowed to survive. There are numerous descriptions of his own playing, but the sum of them suggests no more than the merest shadow of his style. As for the precise nature of *rubato* playing, that has been and will ever remain an unanswerable question. *Rubato* cannot be taught. The student can be told that the word, as applied to timekeeping, means " robbed time " ; that it indicates a device whereby one note is shortened so that another can be lengthened ; that it implies a strict keeping of accounts, and, whenever Peter is robbed, Paul must be fully paid ; that the player (or singer) who forgets to pay his debts in this matter is abusing a great privilege. Beyond this no teacher can go, except by letting the student hear gramophone records of Chopin's music played by a master of the style.

If there is one thing above all else that Chopin teaches us, it is that the whole of music depends upon the adjustment of rhythmic impulse to melodic line. The highest development of a musical mind combines a perception of " pregnant moments " with the power to convey this perception in a perfectly balanced manner. Most of us can be taught to develop a sense of balance, but that peculiar perceptive power is rare, being inborn.

Rubato, like good manners and good taste, is primarily a matter of instinct. If the student does not possess the instinct, no amount of training will evolve it. It were better by far that he should make no attempt to reproduce it and so

avoid that pernicious process which is called " rag-
ging the time." The *rubato* style so far from being
rag-time, is based upon an acute sense of time-
values, and is an eloquent example of the con-
sistency of freedom with law and order. The
proper interpretation of Chopin's music depends,
not upon affected sentimentality, but upon that
larger freedom. And here again we find his music
in strange contrast with the circumstances of his
pitifully entangled life.

For nearly ten years he had been unacquainted
with freedom ; and now that the chains were
broken and his friends were hoping to find a way
of escape, his spirit was crushed by the ever-
increasing weight of disease. At this time (1847)
he was unable to move upstairs without great
pain. He rarely walked. If he had business at
Schlesinger's, he drove there and stayed in his
carriage while one of the assistants came out to
interview him. He summoned strength enough,
however, to give a concert in Paris on February
16, 1848. For this, tickets were sold at extravagant prices and could not be obtained without
influence. The irony of it !

An article in the *Gazette musicale* describes the
brilliant success of the occasion : " Besides the
aristocracy of elegant women, there was present
the aristocracy of artists and amateurs, happy to
catch this sylph of music on the wing. . . . The
sylph kept his word, and with what success, what
enthusiasm ! It is easier to tell you of the welcome he received, and the ecstasies he aroused,
than to describe, analyse and reveal the mysteries
of an execution which has not its like in our
earthly sphere."

A week later came the Revolution and the ab-
dication of King Louis-Philippe, whose reign had
almost exactly coincided with the period of
Chopin's residence in Paris. It was now the
composer's turn to think of abdicating. One of
his pupils, Jane Wilhelmina Stirling, a rich and
talented Scotswoman living in Paris, urged him
to go to England. He took her advice, arrived
in London on April 21, took apartments in
Dover Street, and gave two concerts, the first at
Lord Falmouth's house, the second at the house
of Mrs. Sartoris. He also played at evening
parties, and once, at the Duchess of Sutherland's
house, before the Queen. These occasions brought
him a substantial reward. He then travelled to
Scotland and stayed with Jane Stirling's brother-
in-law, Lord Torpichen, at Calder House ; from
there to Keir, where the Stirling family lived, and
to Johnston Castle. In spite of the fact that his
health was declining every day, he gave concerts
at Manchester, Glasgow and Edinburgh. He returned to London in November, and at the
beginning of 1849 was back in Paris. Delacroix
called to see him and found him in an extremity
of pain and lassitude.

Chopin's letters from England reveal his quiet
self-possession as he moved through the alien
world of London Society. To his family he wrote
at great length, and his comments upon the per-
sonalities and conditions of the period are always
enlightening. A passage from a letter written in
August 1848 is of interest to English musicians :
" After my matinées many papers had good
criticisms, excepting *The Times* in which a certain
Davison writes (a creature of poor Mendel-

ssohn's) ; he does not know me, and imagines, I
am told, that I am an antagonist of Mendelssohn.
It does not matter to me. Only, you see, everywhere in the world people are actuated by something else than truth." We can take comfort
in the thought that our little world of music was
then no more enlightened, no less divided against
itself, than it has been in our own generation.
One page of the same letter carries a footnote :
" The Queen, who has come back to town after
some hostile demonstrations by the opposition,
was to have attended grand opera for a first public
appearance, and the occasion chosen was the first
appearance of Jenny Lind, who also had just
arrived; so there was an enormous rush for tickets.
On the first evening, stalls were sold at three
guineas. . . . On reaching home I found a ticket
for one of the best stalls, from Lumley, the con-
ductor, with the compliments of Miss Lind and
Mrs. Grote. The performance was most magnificent. The Queen received more applause than
Jenny Lind. They sang ' God save ' with the
whole audience standing, and Wellington and all
the local notabilities. It was an imposing sight,
that real respect and reverence for the throne,
for law and order ; they could not contain their
enthusiasm." Later occurs another reference to
Jenny Lind : " Miss Lind came to my concert !
– which meant a lot for the fools. She cannot
show herself anywhere without people turning
their opera-glasses on her. . . . She is not pretty,
but pleasant-looking at home. On the stage I
don't always like her, but in *Sonnambula,* from the
middle of the second act, she is perfectly beautiful in
every and all respects as an actress and as a singer."

Poor Chopin found life in Scotland very boring ; but his letters are full of amusing observation. To Grzymala he wrote : " One of the great ladies here, in whose castle I spent a few days, is regarded as a great musician. One day ... they brought a kind of accordion, and she began with the utmost gravity to play on it the most atrocious tunes. What would you think ? Every creature here seems to me to be a little mad. Another lady, showing me her album, said : ' La reine a regardé dedans et j'ai été à côté d'elle.' A third, that she is ' la 13me cousine de Marie Stuart.' Another sang a French-English romance, accompanying herself on the piano and standing up for the sake of originality. The Princess of Parma told me that one lady whistled for her with a guitar accompaniment. Those who know my compositions ask me : ' Jouez-moi votre second Soupir – j'aime beaucoup vos cloches.' And every remark ends with ' like water,' meaning that it flows like water. I have not yet played to any Englishwoman without her saying to me, ' Like water ' ! They all look at their hands and play the wrong notes with much feeling. Eccentric folk, God help them ! " He appreciated how kind and well-meaning these good people were, and, ill as he was, suffered their attentions with the utmost patience, even when they desired to discuss religion : " Apart from all else, my kind Scottish ladies are wearying me again. Mrs. Erskine, who is a very religious Protestant, good soul, would perhaps like to make a Protestant of me ; she brings me the Bible, talks about the soul, quotes the Psalms to me ; she is religious, poor thing, and she is greatly concerned about

my soul. She is always telling me that the other
world is better than this one ; and I know all that
by heart."

It is for such glimpses as these that we are in-
debted to the relations and friends who preserved
the letters they received from Chopin. Not all
took care to do so. Some did not think of attach-
ing any value to the letters. Others destroyed a
correspondence that was full of intimate secrets,
and it is probable that some of the letters that
Chopin received met a similar fate. According
to one story, Alexandre Dumas *fils* discovered by
chance the complete file of letters written by
George Sand to Chopin. That was in 1851.
Dumas restored the file to George Sand and saw
her burn the letters after reading them through
again. It is certain that fire destroyed other
valuable letters and relics when, in 1863, the
house of Mme Barcinska, Chopin's youngest
sister, was burnt down. A collection of the letters
written by Chopin was made by Henryk Opienski,
and these have been translated into English by
Mrs. Voynich. Her task was made more than
ordinarily difficult by the fact that Chopin sometimes wrote in a French-Polish idiom ; other
letters, which were originally written in French,
make their way into English by way of Polish ;
and again, some of the early letters were found in a
schoolboy jargon of French, German and Latin,
transliterated into Polish.

After his return to Paris in 1849, Chopin still
had strength enough to communicate with his
friends, but for little else. He was compelled to
give up his lessons, and with them a good part of
his income. He had never given very much at-

tention to the state of his finances, and at this
time would have been in great distress had not
Miss Stirling heard of his condition and sent him
money. He was helped, too, in the renting of a
new and splendid apartment. At the beginning
of the summer he left the Square d'Orléans and
took second-floor rooms in the Rue de Chaillot
whence he could look upon a panorama of Paris.
Out of kindness his friends deceived him as to the
cost of these rooms. They gave him a figure which
was half the actual sum ; the Countess Obrzeskow
paid the rest.

In June, Chopin had so strong a presentiment
of the end that he wrote to his sister Ludwika,
begging her to come to him. He was careful not
to alarm her, but it is not difficult to see that his
optimism was forced. Without knowing the reason
he had a sudden great longing to see Ludwika.
No doctor could help him as she could. If funds
were lacking, let her borrow, and when he recovered he would repay. If the family council
would consent to let her come, who could say
whether he would not be able to bring her back
to them himself ! And then, what happiness !

Ludwika came to him without delay and found
that her worst fears were confirmed. Through
the summer months he gradually declined until
even the slightest conversation fatigued him. And
the better part of music's consolation had been
taken away, for he no longer had the strength to
compose or improvise at the pianoforte. With the
coming of autumn, his friends moved him to
another apartment at 12 Place Vendôme. At this
time he could not stand without support, and
Ludwika and his pupil Gutmann were his con-

stant attendants. A few weeks before, his old friend Tytus Woyciechowski arrived in Ostend, and the two tried to arrange a meeting. But even then Chopin was quite unable to travel, and, since Tytus could not obtain a permit to enter France, the plan fell through. " I wanted to go to Valenciennes by train to embrace you," Chopin wrote. " But a few days ago I couldn't get as far as Ville d'Avraye, near Versailles, to my god-daughter, and the doctors will not let me leave Paris. It's my fault for being ill ; otherwise I would have met you somewhere in Belgium. Perhaps you will manage to get here, though I am not selfish enough to demand that you should come here for me. I am so weak that you would have only a few hours of boredom and disappointment alternating with a few hours of pleasure and good memories ; and I should like the time that we spend together to be only a time of complete happiness."

This was one of Chopin's last letters. Another was written to Franchomme who had just gone away in search of sunshine for his health. Chopin, who had not even the desire so to venture, wistfully turned his thoughts to his friend in Touraine. Three doctors had just had a consultation and had forbidden him to move from Paris. He was fully aware of his condition and yet was strangely unperturbed. Indeed, he was looking forward to seeing Franchomme during the winter " under excellent conditions." But after a few sentences a heavy sigh escapes : " How I should like to spend a few days with you all ! "

It is to Charles Gavard, whose sister was one of Chopin's pupils, that we owe an account of the

composer's end. Gavard frequently came to read
to the dying man, who was especially happy in
renewing acquaintance with Voltaire's *Dictionnaire
Philosophique*. The mind was still alert but the
ebb of physical strength could not be stayed, and
at the beginning of October he was unable to sit
up except with the strong arms of Gutmann to
support him. Another of his pupils, and a brilliant one, Princess Marceline Czartoryska, who
had nursed him when he first arrived from
Nohant, again undertook these duties and devoted
the greater part of the day to him. Franchomme
returned from the country. In the room next to
that where Chopin lay, friends and relations
assembled every day. They knew now that this
broken man, whom they loved so well, would soon
be gone from them, and they wished to be near to
warm him with their affection. For all his soli-
tariness, Chopin had always relied heavily upon
his friends, and it is a comforting thought that they
were at hand when he most needed them.

The Abbé Jelowicki called at the apartment in
the hope of seeing him. Chopin and he had been
acquainted in childhood but without being on the
best of terms. Three times the Abbé was refused
admittance ; but when Chopin heard that he had
called, he expressed a wish to see him. Lest the
omission should pain his mother, he did not wish
to die without having received the Sacraments,
" but," he warned the Abbé, " I do not understand them as you require." The Abbé returned
every day. On October 13 Chopin confessed and
made his Communion ; then, embracing the
Abbé, said : " Thank you, friend. Thanks to you
I shall not die like a pig." Soon after, he was

overtaken by fits of suffocation and the final agony began. There came a respite on October 15, when his friend, the Countess Delphine Potocka, arrived from Nice. This beautiful woman, who had once confessed to the composer that life for her was one long dissonance, was now needed to create one harmonious moment before the full close. Chopin asked her to sing. The piano was pushed to the threshold of his room, and, although it was broken by weeping, he heard the lovely voice again. We do not know what was sung. But we can try to imagine what the sound of singing meant to that stricken figure who from the earliest years had been a lord of melody.

Perhaps his life would have ended that day but for that brief interlude. Something in him, we may think, refused to die as long as music could be touched. But the next day he was unable to speak and soon lost consciousness. When he recovered, he was haunted by terrible fears and made a sign that he wished to set down a message. They brought him paper and a pencil, and he wrote : " As this cough will choke me, I implore you to have my body opened so that I may not be buried alive." Later in the day his voice weakly returned and he spoke of his compositions, begging his friends to let no unfinished work be published. Then to each of them he bade farewell. During the night they all kept watch while the Abbé Jelowicki said the prayers for the dying. Their vigil ended in the early hours of the morning.

On October 30, thirteen days after his death, Chopin's funeral took place at the Madeleine. The music of the service included some of his own

works, an orchestration of the Funeral March
from the Pianoforte Sonata in B flat minor, and,
on the organ, two of the Preludes. It was
Chopin's own wish that the music of the Requiem
should be Mozart's, and the request, incidentally,
linked his funeral service with Beethoven's ; for
Lablache, who sang the *Tuba Mirum,* had sung
the same music at that other service twenty-two
years before. Four friends were Chopin's pall-
bearers : Prince Alexander Czartoryski, Delacroix, Franchomme and Gutmann, and the procession was led by Meyerbeer. The other soloists
in the Requiem were Pauline Viardot, Mme
Castellan and Alexis Dupont. The orchestra of
the Conservatoire and a special choir joined in the
performance, which was conducted by Giraud.
The organist, Lefébure-Wély, played the Preludes
during the Offertory. One was the sixth, in B
minor, an echo of Valdemosa. Hearing it, a few,
perhaps, in that congregation called to mind how
often Chopin had looked on death.

After the service the procession moved to the
cemetery of Père Lachaise where Chopin was
buried. But not his heart : that was carried back
to Warsaw to rest in the Church of the Holy
Cross. No formal eulogy was spoken at the burial.
But for the last gesture Chopin would have been
grateful. After his body had been lowered into
the grave, somebody threw earth upon the coffin
from a silver cup. It was the cup of Polish soil
that Elsner and other friends had given him when
they accompanied him to Wola to say good-bye.

LIST OF CHOPIN'S WORKS

Works published posthumously are marked with an asterisk*.
Those to whom Chopin dedicated his works are named in brackets.
All works are for solo piano except where otherwise stated.

Opus
No.

1 Rondo, C minor (Mme de Linde).
2 " Là ci darem " Variations, with orchestra (T. Wojciechowski).
3 Introduction and Polonaise in C (piano and 'cello)
   (J. Merk).
4 *Sonata, C minor (Jozef Elsner).
5 Rondo in the style of a Mazurka (Countess de Moriolles).
6 Four Mazurkas (Countess Plater).
7 Five Mazurkas (Mr. Johns).
8 Trio (piano, violin and 'cello) (Prince Radziwill).
9 Three Nocturnes (Mme Camille Pleyel).
10 Twelve Études (Liszt).
11 First Concerto, E minor, with orchestra (M. Kalkbrenner).
12 Variations, with orchestra, on a rondo from Hérold's
    Ludovic (Miss E. Horsford).
13 Fantasia on Polish airs (M. J. P. Pixis).
14 Krakoviak Rondo, with orchestra (Princess Czartoryska).
15 Three Nocturnes (F. Hiller).
16 Rondo, E flat (Mlle Caroline Hartmann).
17 Four Mazurkas (Mme Lina Freppa).
18 Grande Valse, E flat (Miss L. Horsford).
19 Bolero (Countess de Flahault).
20 First Scherzo, B minor (M. T. Albrecht).
21 Second Concerto, F minor, with orchestra (Countess
    Potocka).
22 Polonaise, E flat, with orchestra (Baroness d'Est).
23 First Ballade, G minor (Baron Stockhausen).
24 Four Mazurkas (Count de Perthuis).
25 Twelve Études (Countess d'Agoult).
26 Two Polonaises (M. J. Dessauer).
27 Two Nocturnes (Countess Apponyi).
28 Twenty-four Preludes (M. Pleyel).
29 Impromptu, A flat (Countess Lobau).

*Opus
No.*

30   Four Mazurkas (Princess of Württemberg).

31   Second Scherzo, B flat minor (Countess von Fürstenstein).

32   Two Nocturnes (Baroness Billing).

33   Four Mazurkas (Countess Mostowska).

34   Three Valses (Mlle de Thun-Hohenstein, Mme G. d'Ivri, Mlle A. d'Eschtal).

35   Sonata, B flat minor.

36   Impromptu, F sharp.

37   Two Nocturnes.

38   Second Ballade, F major (R. Schumann).

39   Third Scherzo, C sharp minor (A. Gutmann).

40   Two Polonaises (J. Fontana).

41   Four Mazurkas (E. Witwicki).

42   Valse, A flat.

43   Tarantella.

44   Polonaise, F sharp minor (Princess de Beauvau).

45   Prelude, C sharp minor (Princess Czernicheff).

46   Allegro de Concert (Mlle F. Müller).

47   Third Ballade, A flat (Mlle P. de Noailles).

48   Two Nocturnes (Mlle L. Duperré).

49   Fantasia, F minor (Princess de Souzzo).

50   Three Mazurkas (L. Szmitkowski).

51   Impromptu, G flat (Countess Esterhazy).

52   Fourth Ballade, F minor (Baroness C. de Rothschild).

53   Polonaise, A flat.

54   Fourth Scherzo, E major (Mlle J. de Caraman).

55   Two Nocturnes (Miss J. W. Stirling).

56   Three Mazurkas (Miss C. Maberly).

57   Berceuse (Mlle Elise Gavard).

58   Sonata, B minor (Countess de Perthuis).

59   Three Mazurkas.

60   Barcarolle (Baroness Stockhausen).

61   Polonaise Fantaisie (Mme A. Veyret).

62   Two Nocturnes (Mlle R. de Konneretz).

63   Three Mazurkas (Countess Czosnowska).

64   Three Valses (Countess Potocka, Baroness de Rothschild, Baroness Branicka).

65   Sonata, G minor, piano and 'cello (A. Franchomme).

66   *Fantaisie Impromptu.

67   *Four Mazurkas.

Opus
No.

68   *Four Mazurkas.

69   *Two Valses.

70   *Three Valses.

71   *Three Polonaises.

72   *Nocturne, E minor, Marche Funèbre in C minor, and Three Ecossaises.

73   *Rondo for two pianos in C major.

74   *Seventeen Polish Songs with piano accompaniment.

Without Opus Numbers.

Three Études.

*Mazurkas in G, B flat, D, C and A minor.

*Valses, E major and minor.

*Polonaises, G sharp minor and B flat minor.

*Variations in E, " The Merry Swiss Boy."

Duo Concertante for piano and 'cello on themes from *Robert the Devil* (written with Franchomme).

Three Valses from the Elsner MSS.

Prelude in A flat major.

Variation VI from the *Hexameron.*

Variations on the March from *I Puritani*; other variations by Liszt, Thalberg, Czerny, etc.

A SHORT BIBLIOGRAPHY

THE following are suggested as a basis for further study :

F. Liszt : *F. Chopin*. Breitkopf (1852 : 6th edition, 1923).

M. Karasowski : *Chopin ; His Life and Letters*. Reeves (1879).

F. Niecks : *F. Chopin as a Man and a Musician*. Novello (1888).

George Sand : *Histoire de ma vie*. Calmann-Lévy.

E. Ganche : *Frédéric Chopin, sa vie et ses œuvres*. Mercure de France (1913).

H. Bidou : *Chopin*. Allen & Unwin (1926).

G. de Pourtalès : *Chopin*. Thornton Butterworth.

H. Opienski : *Chopin's Letters* (English translation by Mrs. Voynich). Desmond Harmsworth (1931).

W. Murdoch : *Chopin: his Life*. Murray (1934).